NEWS

THE WAR REPORT

KING BENJAMIN

VD Style Publishing, LLC

This is a VD Style Publication

THE WAR REPORT Copyright © 2014 by King Benjamin

Cover design: Mario Patterson

Editor: Tina Nance

Interior design and typesetting: InteriorBookDesigns.com

Connect with King Benjamin:

Facebook: Author King Benjamin

Twitter: @kbwordplayz

ISBN 978-0-692-02231-3

I'm dedicating this book to myself and to all those who believed in me and have supported me from the beginning. I'm also dedicating this book to everyone who dares to dream big. Impossible is nothing. I wrote this book from a cell with dreams of being an independent author and publisher, and here I am. Last, but not least, this book is dedicated to my crew who has my back no matter what. Detroit Authors Alliance: Lakelia Blackbyrd Deloach, India T Norfleet, Kenya Rivers, Danielle Marcus and Shanaetriis Jones. DAA for life!

King Benjamin Introduction

So, the way the story goes, or at least the way it was told to me, is that back in the day around 1999, Bones and his brother, Dontae, robbed Mercedes Jay for two kilos of cocaine. It was supposed to be a regular transaction at the same location, just as they had done a hundred times before. Maybe that's why it happened. Maybe Bones and Dontae felt stagnated dealing with Jay, and decided to up the stake and lay a paper play down. Anyway, the way the story goes, E was there with Jay, and both wound up duct taped and stretched out on the floor. No one saw the brothers after that, and it was rumored that they had relocated to Ohio and came up big with the drugs they took from Jay. So, when Dontae was found dead six years later in Detroit, the streets just assumed they knew who was behind it. But I don't know nothing. You ain't heard nothing from me.

CHAPTER 1

"Yes! Yes! Oh God, Jay. Yes!"

Jay's face was buried inside her pretty brown D cup melons as he gripped her soft, juicy bottom and plunged inside her with a hypnotic rhythm and fierce tenacity. He focused on the comfort of her walls as all the worry of the trial, which had begun to unhinge him, temporarily faded away. Sex was his meditation, and as he dug deeper inside her, he tugged her hair with both hands until her neckline was exposed. Like a hungry mad man, he mauled her neck, sucking and biting as he felt her body jolt and her legs shoot straight up in the air.

She began to shudder.

"Ooooh, Ooooh shit!"

Her flowing juices brought him to the peak of a long building climax that erupted into his condom. The feeling was so good; he had to wonder if his condom had broken as he savored his last few strokes before pulling out and turning over. *If this was my last piece of pussy, it was a good fuck*, he thought to himself.

For several minutes, they lay next to each other recovering in silence, with the exception of their heavily thumping hearts. They had been at it a since last night, only taking in a few hours of sleep. Now that it was over, Jay had no choice but to face reality. Without any words to his companion, he rose from the hotel bed and headed for the shower. He was thankful that she was there to comfort him, but honestly, she was just another piece of ass.

He turned on the shower as he contemplated when was the last time he'd met a girl who had any real substance to her character. He couldn't recall. They all wanted the notoriety that came with dating a boss like Mercedes Jay, as he was widely known, but none of them matched his nobility.

Today was the big day, but then again, so was yesterday. His shoulders weighed a ton as he tried to maintain his composure. The jury was about to start the second day of deliberations in a murder trial that had been the basis of his entire existence for the past ten months. The hot steamy shower was therapeutic to his mind and body, so he lingered around for some time after he was done showering. Only when he realized he hadn't heard from his co-defendant and right hand man, Gunner, did he decide to exit the shower. He came out of the bathroom in a towel and gave his booty call a head gesture that let her know the shower was open and he wanted her to get cleaned up and dressed.

His Timex watch read 7:50am and court started at 9:00am. He refused to wear his presidential Rolex to court for the jury to speculate more than they already would, unlike Gunner, who showed up every time looking like a guilty verdict waiting to happen. He called up Gunner to make sure he was up and ready for the day. His girlfriend, Kelly, answered the phone.

"Hello."

"Good morning, Kelly."

"Hey, Jay, how you feeling, babe?"

"I'm feeling pretty good. I just got it in with my one thang, ya dig," he teased, trying to make light of the situation.

"Boy, you is crazy," Kelly said tickled to death. "Here go Keith."

"What up?" Gunner said. Although Gunner sounded as if he'd just woke up, Jay knew Gunner's voice was always exceptionally groggy, so there was no way to know for sure, unless he asked.

"You up, playboy?"

"Hell yeah, I haven't been able to sleep."

"I know, man, me either. But we gonna be aiight though, you know?"

"Fasho. I'm 'bout to gone get dressed, my nigga. I'll see you in a minute."

"Bet."

Jay sounded confident, but he was truly more uncertain than he'd ever been in his whole life. His mind drifted off into a world of what ifs, and was only brought back when the young lady exited the bathroom wearing jeans and a lace bra.

She marched over and stood glaring down at him as he sat on the edge of the bed. "I hope you don't disappear again and don't call me for another month," she said, wearing her 'I mean business' face.

"Baby girl, don't worry about that. I'ma holla at you. After last night, you shouldn't even have to ask," he said.

Jay had only met her a few months ago, and had never even told her about his lingering murder trial. She was nobody, and he didn't feel the information would change anything, so it was pointless. She finished dressing and they parted with a hug and her placing a small kiss on Jay's cheek. It was only after she left that he realized how little he actually knew about her.

Since he was already downtown, he figured he had time to turn in his room key and maybe still get a bite to eat before heading to Frank Murphy Hall of Justice, where his future would most likely be determined today.

~~~

Jay and Gunner arrived at the courthouse about five minutes apart. Gunner was dressed in a grey Armani suit with dark Armani shades and matching shoes. The suit made his shoulders even broader than they were, and the heel on the loafers gave his 5'10" frame another half inch. Gunner had mocha brown skin and a shadow beard that added maturity to his face as he approached his late twenties. His barber always did a good job of concealing his receding hairline, the only thing he was ever self-conscious about.

Kelly gripped his hand, trying to keep up with the fast pace of his walk through the lobby. Her long silky hair bounced off her shoulders and her black ruffled skirt clung to her thighs, rising with each step, as she matched the sense of urgency in her man's stride.

"Vandyke down!" he heard a familiar voice yell.

That stopped Gunner in his tracks as he was about to reach the elevator. He looked back and saw his man, Lines, had just come through the metal detectors, followed by Bake, E and J-Rock. He stormed back toward Lines as he saw that security about to approach and complain about the noise.

"I got him," he said, holding a hand at security. The man nodded as Gunner met up with Lines in the middle of the lobby.

"What's up, my nigga, you good?"

"Nigga, you can't be yelling no shit like that out up here, where you think you at?"

"Man, fuck these crackers. I'ma made nigga," Lines rebutted as he grabbed his dick and bopped through the lobby, meaning every word of it. As the rest of the crew caught up with them, they all gave pounds and hugs to Gunner before heading toward the elevator.

Inside the courtroom, they quickly spotted Jay's tall dark frame already at the defense desk conversing with one of their lawyers. When Jay spotted Gunner, he couldn't help but shake his head at his friend's naivety. Throughout the entire trial, Jay thought he looked a lot less like a murderous drug dealer than his friend did. Jay wore no jewelry, just a three piece Joseph A. Banks suit and Prada loafers, along with a Timex watch.

Sitting a few feet away from him, Gunner rocked a thirty thousand dollar Rolex and a seven thousand dollar pinky ring. What could he say? Gunner was his own man. On the outside looking in, it appeared that Gunner was the boss, but truthfully, there was no boss. Keith and Jason were childhood friends with a mutual respect for each other. If it wasn't for Gunner's excessive gambling and spending habits, he'd have just as much money as Jay. However, being that Jay was the one who had accumulated the most financial security, the whole crew moved under his command, with everyone making the team's well-being a top priority.

Jay cracked a smile as his favorite cousin, Neicey Girl, entered the courtroom, but his smile was quickly erased when the family of the victim, Dontae, family entered the courtroom seconds later. Jay and Gunner were both free on one hundred and fifty thousand dollar bonds. That alone raised the eyebrows of those following the case. None of the victim's family had bothered to attend the trial, but they all showed up for the verdict, praying that the men they believed had taken their loved one away would suffer the harshest penalty available; life without the possibility of parole.

As the jury went into deliberation for the second day, Jay wondered if Dontaes's family had skipped out on the trial out of fear or lack of concern.

"Stanking bitch," he mumbled, as he shot a cold stare at Dontae's sister, Trina.

She was the only reason they were even arrested in the first place. Telling the police that Jay and Gunner had a contract on her brothers' heads, and being the lone witness that claimed to see Jay's navy blue Benz hauling ass out of the gas station parking lot right after the shooting had been enough to secure a warrant. Police were able to place them at the scene, but no other evidence was brought forth linking them to the actual shooting.

They took it to trial and his lawyer argued that anybody would have taken off in hurry under the circumstances. He argued that although his license plate matched the description given to police, and he and Gunner were videotaped inside the station, no one could swear under oath to seeing them actually shoot anyone. Now, his fate lay in the hands of twelve strangers, and he wondered if it was all worth it as his mind drifted back to the night the whole beef started.

It was 1998, and Jay and E lay face down in the weight house hog-tied with duct tape. Their situation was the result of putting too much trust in the wrong niggas. He had let Bones and Dontae see too much. He had let them get too comfortable with his crew. They had made a lot of money together, but it seemed that this was in the plans all along.

"You bitch niggas better hope we find what we looking for," Dontae barked, wielding a Mac-11 as he and Bones ransacked the house.

Jay swore that if he made it out alive, he'd kill them both, no matter how long it took. It was the first and only time he ever feared for his life, but he never forgot the feeling.

He was brought back to the present by his lawyer's voice.

"Hey guys, how you holding up?" Jay heard him say.

Dan Marsh was one of the most recognizable names in Michigan when it came to criminal defense. He was a short stocky man who was half-Italian, and favored the actor, Dustin Hoffman. He was a man of results, but his suits looked straight off the rack, and his shoes appeared to have been worn to every single court appearance for the last three years.

"I'm holding up," Jay assured him.

"I'm good," Gunner said, always the cool head.

Dan had another lawyer from his firm helping with the case, but he was doing almost all the cross-examination.

"Well, listen guys," he said as he motioned for the two of them to huddle up with him. "I just wanna say, I know you're probably a little frustrated with playing the waiting game here, but I gotta tell ya, the longer this jury deliberates, the more I like our chances. The longer this thing plays out, it's more likely that this verdict is gonna come back in your favor. Umm, like I stated several times already, I really don't think the prosecution has proven this case beyond a reasonable doubt. So, when the jury steps back into this room, I don't wanna see any long faces. Show no fear. I want you to look as if you expect to be exonerated."

If nothing else, the pep talk had Jay and Gunner feeling more optimistic than they had five minutes before it. Dan's mouthpiece was his money. He was very convincing, and Jay believed he was worth every penny they had spent to hire him.

~~~

Bones had waited six years for this. After completing the mandatory six of his twelve-year sentence for a second degree murder charge in Ohio, he was finally free to go. From all observations and information, it seemed that

Bones was born with a black heart. Prison had only made him colder. Bones was twenty-nine years old, and he got his name from his tall, lanky frame and always being so frail growing up. His skin was black like coal, and his eyes were constantly bloodshot red, even when he was stone sober. As time passed, Bones' nickname was thought to be in reference to the dead bodies he'd accumulated throughout his stint on the streets. Of course, Bones never clarified were the name came from, leaving most to make their own assumptions.

He had no plans to stick around in Ohio, his time was done and he wanted out. His plan was to get the parole transferred to his hometown of Detroit, Michigan, but if the plans took longer than he expected, he would say fuck parole all together and just leave. Bones had revenge, money and murder on his mind, and he was itching to get back to the place where he could make it happen. He knew who was responsible for his brother, Dontae's death. If Mercedes Jay was lucky enough to beat the charge, he'd be waiting around the corner to deal him and his whole Vandyke crew his own brand of justice. As Bones sat up in the control center waiting, still wearing prison clothes, his mind traveled back to his darkest day; the day he got the word of Dontae's death.

"I have something to tell you, but I need you to promise me you won't lose it in there, okay?" his sister Trina had said, knowing Bones was going to flip.

"What's wrong?"

"Bones, promise me you will try your best to handle this, okay? We need you to come home, so just please promise me, okay?"

"Man, just tell me what happened." Bones ordered.

"Dontae was shot five times last night at the gas station. He's dead, Bones."

Bones banged the phone against the wall, cracking the receiver. He could hear his sister screaming his name as he walked away from the phone station.

Bones knew who had killed his brother; everybody knew. Twice in the head, once in the neck, and two in the shoulder. He contemplated how he would administer pain to the first of many that would feel his wrath. His only regret was not killing Jay and E when he had a chance. It was Dontae's idea to let them live. But for the life of him, he didn't understand what had made Dontae go back to Detroit and not take care of the unfinished business. They had come up off the two keys they took from Jay, but the word on the streets was that the two keys was like chump change to Jay now. Bones didn't care about Jay's money; he was out for blood.

~~~

The word came back in two hours in that there was a verdict. Jay took in a deep breath as the overweight court bailiff began to speak.

"All rise... the honorable judge Andrew Strong presiding. You maybe be seated."

As the Caucasian judge in his late fifties took the chair and straightened his glasses, Jay peeked back at his crew one last time. They looked more nervous than he was. E was stroking his three sixty waves obsessively. Lines was biting his nails and bouncing one knee up and down on the floor, while Bake sat with one elbow on each thigh stroking his goatee. J-Rock sat with his head down, and he looked as if he was praying.

The female foreperson handed the bailiff a small folded paper, and the bailiff hobbled up to the judge to pass it along.

"Has the jury reached a verdict?"

"Yes we have, your honor," the foreperson said, standing extremely erect.

"How do you find?"

"In the case of the people vs. Jason Burks and Keith Randall, on the charge of First Degree Murder, we the people find the defendants, not guilty."

Mixed reactions rippled through the crowd from the victim's family along and Jay and Gunner's family and friends. The judge banged the gavel in order to silence the courtroom, and the foreperson continued.

"In the case of the people vs. Jason Burks and Keith Randall, on the charge of Felony Possession of a Firearm, we the people, find the defendants not guilty."

Continued gasps and cheers were allowed after the full verdict was read, but the judge banged his gavel again, once the courtroom seemed to be in an uproar.

"Order! Order!"

Jay's crew looked on, mean mugging the family of the victim as they left the court spewing derogatory language at the jury. Jay and Gunner embraced Dan, and the three of them patted each other on the back.

"Good job, Dan, I knew you could do it. I knew you could," Jay said.

"Hey you guys, just stay out of trouble for me, okay? It's no fun having your whole life in the hands of people who don't even know you, ya know what I mean?"

"You right about that," Gunner said. "But enough talking, let's get the fuck outta here."

CHAPTER 2

The first thing the crew did after leaving court was go out for lunch to celebrate the victory. They all met up at Jay's favorite spot, The Parthenon in Greektown. Jay loved the elegance and architecture of the building. The gold and white theme inside was accented by marvelous gold chandeliers and floor to ceiling wall windows out front. Intimate tables for two lined the walls, and the middle aisle boasted several twelve-foot Cherry wood tables like the one Jay and his party of ten occupied.

Along with Kelly and Neicey Girl, a couple of Gunner's personal goons had already joined them at the celebration. Gunner's people were extended members of the family from the Van Dyke neighborhood they had all grown up in. Gunner had goons from all over Charmers,

Mack, even Brightmore. Most of them were cats he knew from prison and had recruited them after realizing they had potential. Whomever Gunner brought in was immediately blessed, because no one doubted his ability to judge character.

Jay was finally able to relax, and he couldn't stop laughing as Bake told another one of his outlandish stripper tales.

"Man, I'm telling you. This bitch had me gone! I'm sitting at home like a fiend talking about, 'baby you ain't gotta go to work today, I got you.' Every night, I'm like, 'baby I got you.' I ain't even paid my mortgage for the month. I done paid this bitch mortgage and car note."

The whole table was crying with laughter as Bake told the truth with a straight face. It was always like this when the crew got together. Bake, with his love for strippers and natural comedic personality, always had a story to tell. He was a short chubby dude who got his name, Shake-n-Bake, because he was a natural chemist when it came to cooking up powdered cocaine and turning it into crack. Bake knew all the tricks of stretching coke, and he always brought back at least forty-two ounces off each kilo. At the most, he could bring back sixty, but there was only a slim chance of the dope being any good. Bake had been the designated cook for the crew, and he was paid one thousand dollars for every kilo he whipped up.

E was Bake's half-brother, but by the looks of them, you'd never know it. E was high yellow with naturally wavy hair, and was considered the ladies' man of the crew. He was average in height and had been labeled a pretty boy in high school. He didn't mind back then, but now days you couldn't call him a pretty boy unless you wanted to engage in a fist fight afterwards.

To his right was J-Rock, the exact opposite of E. There was nothing pretty about J-Rock. He had bad acne ,and the nappiest head of hair you've ever seen. Even with a little money, J-Rock still carried himself with an air of low self-esteem. J-Rock, the youngest of the crew, really looked up to Jay, and aspired to be just like him.

And then there was Lines. The only man in the crew that got high off his own supply. Lines had been sniffing coke since age seventeen, and he was now twenty-five. Lines was a heartless bastard who sold drugs to his mother and threatened her if she didn't pay the money she owed on time. The years of drug use made Lines appear much older than he was. He had cocoa butter skin, and although he was by no means a fat man, you could tell he had never taken any measures to get in shape by the way he was built. He was teased about his man breasts all the time, but Lines was a good earner, and Jay never questioned his loyalty to the crew, not even for a second.

The crew had finished off their meals, and everyone was reclining and sucking their teeth. Jay started to speak in a low tone, almost a whisper, that let everyone know he was about to talk business. He didn't mind Kelly and Neicey Girl hearing what he had to say. They knew everything about the crew's operation already.

"Aye, dig this here, I know we ain't been working too much because of trial and all that, but y'all know we done missed out on a lot of money. It's time to get back to business. Go hard or go home. Ain't no pussy footing around, we gotta get them phones ringing off the hook again, ya dig? I'm going to hook up with my man in the morning to get us right, and then we can meet up at the record store. But tonight..." His voice went up dramatically as he stood to his feet. "Is time to party like a muthafucka, nigga! Tear the club up, nigga! Van Dyke Down, nigga!" he yelled like a teenager with no home training.

"Ayee Van Dyke Down, nigga!" Lines rose to his feet to join in the foolery as they all slapped fives and got hype.

Lines pulled out a bankroll and made it rain on the table for no apparent reason other than dropping bills on top of half-eaten plates.

"Everything on me tonight, nigga," Jay continued. "Bake, call up some of them stripper hoes. Kelly, I'm sorry, but you can't come on this ride, baby," he teased.

"Fuck you, Jay, don't start no shit."

They began to calm down just as the manager was approaching. He saw everyone taking their seats, so he just strolled on by, not wanting any confrontation. The managers loved Jay; he had been a frequent customer for the past five years, ever since he started touching real paper.

Jay had been in the game since the early nineties. He'd had his ups and downs, but now he was finally on top of his game, where he knew he would be. He'd lost some soldiers to the graveyard and the penal system, but the closest people to him were still right by his side. He'd always remember the setback that almost took him completely out of the game, and that was why Dontae had to die. There was no way he could ever let it ride, so when he heard that Dontae had resurfaced, he knew it was only a matter of time.

Gunner was the one who spotted him in his Lexus chilling at the gas station like it was all good that night. Jay pulled over and got out of his Benz at a nearby alley, letting Gunner get behind the wheel. As Dontae dipped in and out of the gas station, he surveyed his surroundings, but Jay was already laying in the cut itching to squeeze like an ass man at a nudie bar.

As Dontae climbed behind the wheel of the Lexus, Jay snuck up from behind, concealing his .40 cal until he was at point blank range.

Then he opened fire.

CHAPTER 3

B ones decided that the first thing he needed to do was take a trip back to Detroit, and get his business in order. He had a million things to do, but he knew what came first on the list. Although he intended to murder, maim, and destroy, he also didn't plan to ever go back to prison, so everything had to be calculated and executed to perfection. First order of business was the drugs that had been in Dontae's ex-girlfriend's basement for a year now collecting dust. He needed clothes, a cellphone, and he needed to find his homeboy, Skip. Skip was his right hand, and he had been doing his best to keep tabs on the Van Dyke Down crew. He found out from his sister, Trina, that Jay and Gunner had beat the case, which was music to his ears. Prison was getting off easy as far as he was concerned. He had a better idea.

At the moment, he was stuck in a parole office in Columbus, Ohio, listening to a fat bald white man with thick glasses yapping at the mouth as if he was some sort of tough guy.

"And let me be totally honest. I don't like you, Mr. Simmons. I don't like your kind. I don't like the fact that drug dealing scum like you can go to jail for killing somebody and do half of the time because of some fucking day for day law that should have been thrown out years ago. I'd give my right arm to change that law right now. I swear I'd do it."

"Then you must be left handed," Bones said, smirking at the PO.

He grimaced until the wrinkles in his forehead grew bigger. "You're not fucking funny. And I'm willing to bet you'll be back in prison before the year is out. I want you to get a job immediately, Mr. Simmons, and I wanna see some check stubs by the end of next month. If I don't see check stubs, I wanna see some school enrollment verification or some form of fucking evidence that you're not out here becoming a menace to society all over again."

This guy was real piece of work. If Bones hadn't just come home, he would have already slapped the wire frame glasses clean off his face.

"Are you finished?" Bones said with impatience in his tone.

His PO scowled as if he had been insulted. "You're not fucking tough!" he yelled as he went on another rampage that lasted almost two whole unbearable minutes. "Now get the fuck out of my office!"

After his meeting with Satan, Bones knew he'd never complete a parole with the devil himself as his parole agent. It was downright laughable to think he'd assist him in transferring his parole to Detroit. He knew what he had to do.

~~~

Mercedes Jay stood in the VIP area he had reserved for the Van Dyke Down Crew, looking down on at the dance floor that was filled to capacity. He and Gunner wore matching chains with the initials VD in huge letters flooded with flawless diamonds. Besides his Rolex, the chain was the only expensive piece of jewelry Jay had. He wasn't big on jewelry, but he was big on doing it big. Gunner wore a Jesus piece under his VD chain that he had spent another thirty-five thousand dollars getting iced out. Including his presidential Rolex and pinky ring, he was walking around with over a hundred thousand dollars' worth of jewelry on. They looked like celebrities surrounded by beautiful women and champagne as they celebrated their biggest victory yet.

Jay sat down next to an exotic looking woman Gunner had invited. She wore a pink strapless hip hugging dress that had her breasts spilling out and her thighs waving hello. Jay decided J-Rock didn't look like he was enjoying himself, so he sent two girls over to him with the task of raising his comfort level. Lines was whispering in another girl's ear, and Jay was sure by the grin on his face that he was trying to convince her to sniff some coke with him. Lines was always trying to corrupt somebody.

"You a dirty muthafucka, Lines!" Jay yelled and laughed.

"What I do?" Lines replied, looking innocent.

Jay just shook his head and went on with his conversation. He wasn't a drinker at all, but tonight was too special not to indulge with the fellas, so he cracked a bottle of Cristal for him and the dime piece wearing the hip hugging dress. After three glasses of champagne and a shot of 1738, Jay was toasted. He was standing on the leather sectional that surrounded them in a half circle with his hands in the air rocking to the beat of the music. Young Jeezy's "Trap or Die" was the latest song that had the clubs rocking like a boat in a tropical storm.

"Last time I checked, I was the man on these streets," Jay rapped as the song started.

Some of the girls in their entourage were strippers, and as the beat kicked in, they couldn't resist the urge to bust it wide open and drop it to the floor. Bake and Gunner pulled out stacks of money as if they had come prepared for this moment. As they tossed money in the air once again, all eyes were on the Van Dyke Down crew.

~~~

Michelle sat in her luxury loft in downtown Detroit staring out the window at her view of the neighboring country of Canada as she snacked on a fruit salad. She had enjoyed her day off at home all alone. The People Mover, a train that operated at sky level, came into view, and she could see the faces of some of her local celebrity coworkers on the billboard advertisement for Channel 4 news. Michelle had been working for the local news station for almost four years now, and was beginning to wonder how long it was going to take for her to be promoted from street reporter to her dream job as lead anchor of the nightly news.

She used to enjoy street reporting and turning monotonous stories into attention grabbers. She used to love the thrill of the chase, trying to be first on the scene when a big story broke. Although she was getting much better stories to cover than when she first started, street level reporting had become downright boring and depressing. So much violence in the city, the rape and murders seemed to be never ending. If she was lead anchor, she'd still have to do all those depressing stories, but she would have a chance to pitch some of her ideas on how to show off the positive side of Detroit. She had so many ideas she felt could help bring the city together, but she needed a platform.

The house was still as Michelle turned from her picture window and took a seat on the sofa in her living area. She glanced up at some of her trophies and medals that were displayed on the mahogany mantle, and she began to feel nostalgic as she thought back to her days at Arizona State University, and her friends back in her hometown of Roanoke, North Carolina. Michelle had moved to Michigan after her best friend from college promised her a job at a local news station.

With a small sigh, she set the bowl of fruit on the coffee table then stood up and strolled over to the mantle. A smile danced across her face as she reached out to grab the glass case that held her biggest accomplishment to date; a silver medal she'd won with the US gymnastics team in the 2000 Olympics. It wasn't gold, but it damn sure beat nothing, and she was extremely proud of it. Just being able to make her parents proud of her was worth all the hard work that went into making it all the way the Olympics.

"Accomplishments," she mumbled. "That's what it's all about."

As a sophomore, Michelle was an All Pac-12 first team academic honoree, and led the list of all academic selections for Arizona State. She had been a fixture on the floor and vault lineup since her freshman year, and after the Olympics, she went on to graduate with a degree in broadcast journalism. Accomplishing goals is was she did, but that feeling hadn't been present in years, and she wanted it back. Sure, she could make the argument that she had already accomplished a lot in her twenty-eight years, but it wasn't like her to be stagnant. She needed to see some type of forward progress in her life.

Michelle placed the glass case back on the mantle and headed off to the shower, leaving a trail of pajamas, panties, and her bra all the way to the bathroom. She studied herself in the mirror that covered the entire frame on the back of the bathroom door, taking in the scenery. Her butterscotch skin glowed against her jet-black spiral curls. Michelle still had the amazing body of a gymnast, with muscle definition and womanly curves to make a man drool. It was hard to believe that she was still single, but she told herself repeatedly that she wasn't lonely, and most of the time she believed it. Still, nights like this, she couldn't help but think about all the what ifs.

CHAPTER 4

J ay woke up with the hangover he was expecting. He
lay in the bed trying to muster up the energy to
move, knowing he had business that needed to be
handled. The first attempt to move happened an hour
ago, but the migraine headache told him not to do it, so
he went back to sleep. By now, he was sure his connect
had called him, and more than likely, so had Bake. He
was about to make a promise to never drink again, but he
decided not to keep lying to himself. As he slid out of
bed, he began to feel better as his banging headache
subsided. He turned on his cell phone and it rang
seconds later. He answered it quickly.

"Hello?"

"What up doe?" Bake said.

"Shit, I'm running late. Woke up with a hangover."

"Man, you should've stayed at the hotel. Them hoes got freaky deaky. You know I was like a kid in a candy store, going from room to room. I ran through a box of condoms, nigga, like it wasn't shit."

Jay listened as Bake went on about his escapades from the night before, waiting for a break to cut in and talk business. Jay wasn't into strippers, especially if they wanted to exchange sexual favors for money. He respected the hustle, but tricking was beneath him. He had the old school values of his father, who was a gangster and a pimp from the seventies era.

"Bake," Jay interrupted. "I'ma call you after I hook up with Dog, so we can meet up at Neicey Girl's house."

"Aiight, I'm waiting on you. I'll be here smoking a blunt, watching Maury or some shit."

"Okay, my guy," Jay said chuckling.

After showering and changing into a Sean Jean velour sweat suit, Jay tossed duffle bags in the back of his Yukon Denali and backed out the garage of his St Clair Shores home that sat right off the Detroit River, and headed to meet up with his connect, who was growing impatient.

He thought about his new southwest connect that Lines was about to introduce him to. He couldn't wait for the day he could dump his old connect for the new one. Just because Dawson was the Mayor's son, he thought he was the boss of all bosses, but all that shit was about to change.

~~~

Bones had snuck into the city the night before, and was on his way to meet up with his main man, Skip, who he hadn't seen in seven years, except for pictures that he got in the mail. He made a right on Mansfield and Puritan, feeling good to be back in his old hood. As he got closer to the address Skip had given him, he could see a man being beaten unmercifully on a front porch. The man dropped to his knees then fell on his bottom, held up only by the threshold of the front door.

Bones scratched his head as he peered at the man's attacker. He bore a strong resemblance to Skip. Glancing at the address on the house confirmed that he had reached his destination. He pulled his 98' Cadillac STS over, shaking his head. As he cut the car off and got out, the beating continued as Skip stopped only for a second to see who was in front of his spot.

"Where my money at, bitch? Huh? Where the fuck my money?" Skip raised his left foot and began kicking the man in the stomach until he doubled over, and then Skip continued kicking him in the rib area. "You think I'm playing about my money? Huh?"

Another man stood by, watching the assault as Bones approached the front porch. Skip was brown skinned with big lips. He was average height and less than two hundred pounds, but he packed a punch.

"Damn, you ain't even gonna welcome ya manz back?" Bones asked, unconcerned about the event that was taking place.

"Yeah nigga, hold up," Skip said, breathing heavily. "Where my money at?"

Skip's victim was bleeding all over the front porch, and he seemed to have no answers for Skip, so he continued to be pulverized until Skip could no longer go on.

"Shit, you done got paid now, nigga. Look at all this muthafucking blood on the porch," Bones said as Skip finally walked over and embraced him like a brother.

"Will, go get a mop or something and get that blood up for me. And get that nigga off my porch." Skip ordered one of his young goons as he and Bones began to walk near the sidewalk to have a private conversation.

Neighbors tried their best not to stare, not wanting to cause any confusion with Skip. He wasn't always this messy, so the neighbors tried to mind their business while he went about his.

"Come on, let's hop in the whip for a minute," Skip said as they walked to the Cadillac.

Inside, Skip removed a chrome plated ten-millimeter pistol and handed it to Bones.

"Oooh baby, where you been all my life?" Bones said as he kissed the gun.

"That's yours, nigga, this too," Skip said, handing him a few stacks.

"Good looking out, my nigga. Now, I'll be aiight when I can get up out this old ass Caddy," Bones said.

"Damn nigga, you just got out, slow your ass down."

"Man, you know me. Ain't shit slow about my life."

"True dat," Skip agreed.

"That's your Marauder in the driveway?"

"Yeah, I got that bitch when it first came out. It's time for something else now."

"Don't even worry about it, nigga, we'll be good in minute. I told you I been keeping in touch with Oshiwa right?

"Dontae bitch, yeah," Skip said shaking his head, remembering the conversation.

"Yeah, bitch got five bricks in the basement that my brother left when he died."

"Yeah?"

"Hell yeah, she waiting on me to come get that shit right now."

"That's a down ass bitch right there. You gonna have to show her some love for that."

"No doubt about it," Bones said, slapping fives with Skip."

Skip had been twisting up a blunt from the moment they started the conversation about his car. He finished rolling the weed and passed it to Bones, knowing he was ready to get some smoke in his lungs.

"So, what's the run down on those hoe ass Van Dyke Down niggas?"

"Well shit, you know Jay and Gunner beat the case already. All them niggas out here, but I really can't say what they driving and all that, 'cause I been over here grinding, trying to get shit up and running right. Jay still got that navy blue Benz though."

"Hoe ass nigga keep a Benz," Bones said with hate in his voice.

"What's the nigga name they say be sniffing the coke and shit?"

"Lines?"

"Yeah, that nigga still around. I heard he be wit a li'l young nigga name J-Rock. I don't know what he look like. I never seen him. I had my man on the east side checking on all he could though, so he know it's important. He gonna be getting back with me quick with some more info."

"Don't tell the nigga too much though, or we'll have to clap his ass too when it's all said and done."

"Nah, this my man. He good people. Oh yeah, you remember Carlos? The light skin nigga with the good hair? I think he used to fuck with your sister back in the day."

"Yeah, Los, I remember. What about him?"

"I think we might need him. Cash him out on a couple of them niggas 'cause dog gets busy, you hear me?"

"Los?" Bones said in shock.

"Hell yeah, Los. My nigga Los ain't playing no games out here. For what we trying to do, he's a nigga you want in your corner."

Bones looked at Skip with skepticism in his eyes. Last thing he remembered about Los, he was a compulsive gambler who hustled to support his gambling habit. Now, Skip was telling him he was a well-qualified contract killer.

"Are you sure we talking about the same Los?"

"Yeah nigga, ask your sister. She keep her ear to the street, so I know she heard about him by now."

Bones decided he would do some research on Carlos and see if it was real or not. He'd hate to have to go at Carlos for doing a half ass job or running off with his cash without producing some bodies. But Bones didn't dare underestimate The Vandyke Down crew. He knew Jay had some killers on his squad, and he needed to spread some money around to make sure he had enough soldiers on his team before he went at them. Otherwise, he'd be fighting a losing battle.

~~~

After linking up with his connect, Jay dropped all the work off at Neicey Girl's house and left to get some more baking soda after realizing he was super low. When he got back to the house, he rang the doorbell and she came to the door quickly. Jay could smell the fried chicken she was cooking as soon as he came to through the door. Almost every time Jay came over, she would fry chicken, knowing how much he loved her chicken.

Neicey Girl was short and dark skinned with a beauty mole on her left cheek. Jay often teased her about being single, but the way Jay treated her, all she needed a man for was his dick. Although Jay paid all her bills, in her mind she went to work every day, so she was an independent woman.

The bell rang again as she was putting a scrunchie around her Tyzillions.

"Get the door, Jay," she said.

Jay peeked out of the peep hole and opened the door for Gunner, who came straight in bitching about he'd just lost a few of thousand in a dice game. Neicey Girl had disappeared into the basement, but she reappeared struggling with two loaded duffle bags and threw them on the floor next to Jay's feet.

"Thanks for the help, niggas," she said, being sarcastic.

"Neicey, I'm going in here and get some of this chicken right quick," Gunner said, already half way in the kitchen.

"Go ahead, what you telling me for?"

Jay watched Gunner's every move, thinking he was moving too fast and looking too hungry to be left alone in the kitchen. He knew that Bake would be pulling up in a second and it would be all over. Gunner came out of the kitchen with a loaf of bread and a bottle of hot sauce and placed it on the tray in front of his seat. As he darted back to the kitchen, Jay was on his heels.

"Hold up, you ain't bout to eat up all the chicken, muthafucka!"

~~~

The Channel Six news van bent the corner fast and stopped on a dime as the sliding door flew open. Michelle popped out, headed for the First National Bank. They were first on the scene, but they didn't know if the story had gone live on another channel already. Channel Six news prided themselves on being the first to break all the biggest stories. This was a big one. A bank robbery, hostages, police shootout, and a dead perpetrator killed at the scene.

Michelle felt that adrenaline rush she hadn't had in a while as she scurried to find the lead detective on the scene. As she got closer to the crime scene, he found her first, not wanting her to interfere with the investigation.

"Excuse me officer, where can we set up?" she asked.

"You're gonna have to take it over there, because all of this is still a crime scene."

"Okay, no problem. Real quick, can you tell me any details about what happened here today?"

He was trying to get back to work before she could get it out, knowing what her next question was going to be. He pivoted on his foot and turned back around to give her as much information as he could in a timely manner.

After she was done with the detective, she rushed her cameraman to the set up spot, her Christian Dior heels clacking to a fast rhythm.

"Mike, are you there?" she spoke in her earpiece.

Mike, the technical engineer came in loud and clear. "Yeah, I hear you. Are you all set up?"

She stood holding her microphone and tugging on her suit jacket to make sure she wasn't all wrinkled up on camera. Mike came in again. "You ready?"

A glance at the cameraman and his head nod confirmed that they were ready.

"Yes, we're ready."

"Okay, we're on in five, four, three, two..."

"This is Michelle Mitchell, reporting live from right outside the First National Bank in Taylor, just west of Canal Street, where from what I understand, a brazen armed robbery has taken place. It ended in the worst way for the suspect who was shot and killed by police. Police say the suspect entered the bank around ten pm and immediately produced a high powered assault rifle, taking hostages and demanding one hundred thousand dollars. Police arrived on the scene before he could make get away. Uh... apparently, after several attempts to negotiate with the suspect, he became irate and tried to escape with his gun aimed at one the hostage's head for security. The brave hostage struggled to break free, and once she was out of the line of fire, police opened fire on the suspect. We have confirmed reports that the suspect died on the scene."

The lead anchor for midday news came into Michelle's earpiece.

"Okay, now we're hearing the hostage was actually shot as well. Do you have any confirmation on that? And if so, is she okay?

"Um yes, the hostage was actually grazed in the thigh by the assailant as she struggled to get free. She was taken to the hospital, but I'm told her wounds were superficial and she's will make a full recovery."

"Okay, now have you had a chance to talk to any of the hostages?"

"No I haven't, Jim, the police are still questioning the people who were inside at the time. I'm going to try and see if I can get a statement from some of them as they are permitted to leave."

"Okay, Michelle, we have another breaking news story coming in right now, so we'll check back with you a little later for an update."

"Okay, thanks Jim."

Michelle had some down time while police were interviewing the hostages, so she decided to return her best friend's call who she just realized had called her two days in row. She would never ignore Leslie, she just hadn't seen the missed call.

When Leslie answered the phone, her voice had too much joy in it for it to be bad news.

"Have you been so busy trying to fuck your way to the top that you couldn't call me back?" Leslie teased.

Michelle snatched the phone away from her ear and stared at it before responding. "Bitch, did I dial the wrong number?"

"No you didn't dial the wrong number, bitch, this is Leslie, your best friend who has great news she been trying to tell you for two days."

"Let me guess, you were finally inducted into the hoe hall of fame?"

"Oooh, now I gotta cut cha. That's the rule," Leslie screamed. They both burst into laughter and Michelle just shook her head. Leslie had a way of bringing out a silly ghetto side of Michelle that nobody else could. She never used that kind of language except when she was talking to Leslie.

"So what's the good news?" Michelle asked still giggling.

"I didn't say good news, I said great news. And the great new is Kevin popped the question, and I'm officially engaged to be married."

"OH MY GOD!" Michelle squealed into the receiver. "Congratulations, you finally found someone besides me that wants to keep you around."

"You know what? You ain't gonna ruin my moment. You gotta see this ring. You're probably gonna try and slip it off my hand and sell it for drugs or something."

"Now you see, bitch, I was gonna invite you to dinner to celebrate, but you just killed it with that."

"Yes, we have to celebrate ASAP. When are you off?"

"You know I usually don't come on until the end of the month," she teased.

"Heffa!"

"Okay, okay. I'm off Saturday."

"Good, me too."

"Okay, I'll see you Saturday, and congratulations again. I gotta get back to work."

"Okay. Bye."

CHAPTER 5

T he crew was all there as Jay pulled his Benz up to the back entrance of his record store with Gunner following closely. Damn Good Music had three locations on the east and west side, with the third one just recently opening in Highland Park. The record stores earned good consistent money for Jay, and allowed him a clean paper trail through his bank accounts, but it was nothing like dope money.

He heard the passenger door fling open on Lines' Suburban and it got his attention. A female with wild uncombed hair and old faded jeans exited the truck and took off down the alleyway. Jay shook his head. He didn't see her face, but knew it had to be Deja.

Deja used to be one the coldest chicks the hood had to offer until Lines got a hold to her. He decided he was tired of her coming around smoking up his weed, and him never getting anything out of it but a hard time. One day, he rolled up a blunt and laced it with coke and fed it to her like it was a T-bone steak. In the days that followed, Deja would come back begging for more of the same weed until Lines finally broke the bad news to her. He knew she would be upset, but more than anything, he knew she had a habit.

Now days, Deja had graduated to the pipe, and Lines gets to have her whenever he wants to for a little or nothing. It didn't bother him one bit that he had destroyed a beautiful young girl's future.

Jay's cell phone rang as he was about to get out the car. He saw it was Dawson's number, so he answered.

"Hello?"

"Yo."

"What's up?"

"You like a stack short," Dawson said, referring to the money Jay had just given him.

"A stack short?"

"Yeah."

"You sure?"

"Positive. I ran it through twice. You know the machine ain't gonna lie."

Dawson was a spoiled brat that Jay felt was only selling drugs to fit in. Being from a family that was well to do and politically connected, Dawson could have done anything he wanted with his life. And what was he doing? Supplying the east side of Detroit with drugs.

"If you say so, man. I don't know how that could've happened, but I'll take care of you."

"Okay. No rush, I just wanted you to know about it."

"Aiight, bet."

Jay hung up and went inside the store through the back entrance, where everyone was waiting for him. Lines had made it in just before he had, and was teasing E about having five kids by four baby mothers.

"Lines, you a dirty muthafucka, man. I seen Deja get out your truck," Jay said.

"Man, I was bored. I been waiting around this muthafucka two hours for you to get here."

"So, you figured, 'I'll just get my dick sucked right quick in the back of this nigga shop since he taking so long,' huh?"

"Man, where the work at?" Lines said changing the subject.

"Wait, we still talking 'bout this nigga with four baby mamas," Bake explained.

"You need three or four baby mamas though. Who else gonna hold all your work and put all yo shit in they name?" E justified. "And the best thing about it is I take care of my kids, so I don't gotta give they ass a dime, you feel me?" he finished with a giggle.

"Now you just lying," Gunner commented as he began to pull kilos out of the duffle bag he had brought in.

"Don't front, you know you paying a couple mort-gages around town, muthafucka," Jay agreed.

"Maybe so, but I always got a place to lay my head, and I ain't never chasing after no pussy."

Nobody could deny the two facts E had just stated.

"Wait 'til you fuck up though," Bake said. "I got two words for you. Child support, nigga. Laugh now cry later."

The crew laughed as they started to attend to the business at hand.

~~~

Bones wasted no time in stalking Mercedes Jay and his crew. He had learned that they frequented the record store Jay owned in his old neighborhood, so he parked down the street from the store in front of a restaurant. From his position, he could only see the front of the store and the comings and goings through the front entrance. He sat patiently with malice in his eyes waiting for the a-ha moment that never came.

An hour and a half later, he grew tired of watching customers go in and come out with nothing but what appeared to be legit purchases. He realized that he should have had Skip or somebody else on this part of the job, because he had other shit to do. He decided to come back later after he'd taken care of his other business. He pulled away from the curb, slowly eyeballing the record store like the actual building had done something wrong, when all of a sudden, a procession of cars rolled from the back alley and took off in all different directions. He quickly spotted Jay's Benz with Gunner following behind him in his Audi. Two Cadillacs took off in the same direction, and then a Jeep Cherokee pulled out last.

Bones fell back and lit a cigarette. He drove below the speed limit to ensure that he was not noticed. He decided to stay behind the jeep since he was the only one that didn't have a car tailing him. As the jeep cruised up Van Dyke doing exactly the speed limit, Bones smirked, knowing that the man inside probably had drugs in the car. When the jeep made a left turn, so did Bones, following him another two miles until he pulled into a gas station.

Bones was trailing far enough behind to be able to ride by and get a good look at the man just as he was stepping out of his jeep. It was a young unfamiliar face that fit the description Skip had given him.

"J-Rock," he mumbled. "Yeah, I'ma tear yo fucking head off too, nigga."

He headed toward the freeway to hit Oshiwa's house. His plan was to take Dontae's old Lexus that was still in her name to the dealership before 5:00 to do a trade in.

He had Skip rounding up his people who he felt he could trust to run the new spots they were about to open on the west side. Then, he was going to break bread with the dude that was doing all his research on Mercedes Jay and crew.

When Bones arrived at Oshiwa's house, he had to ring the doorbell a few times before she actually came to the door. She was wearing beige shorts and halter-top that displayed the entire God given blessings of her curvaceous framework. Oshiwa was an average looking girl, with a knock out body. She wore her hair in curls on the top and a short taper. She had just stepped out the shower and gotten dressed when she let Bones in, and he could smell her Victoria Secret Strawberries & Champagne lotion that lingered in the air.

"What's up, my nigga?" she said as the two of them shared a long embrace. It was the first time they'd seen each other in years, although they'd had hundreds of phone conversations since then.

"Good to be back home, you know?" He spoke in his usual slow monotone.

"I'll bet. Hold up a second."

She pushed the remote button on her fifty-five inch plasma and disappeared into her back bedroom. Bones took out his personal weed stash and a blunt. He hadn't had a chance to smoke all day, with trying to stay focus on the duties he had planned for himself. As he split the cigar open with a thumbnail, Oshiwa came out of the bedroom jingling the keys to the Lexus and holding a white business card along with it.

"Aww shit now, you bought me some weed." she said.

"If that's what you choose to believe, be my guest," Bones replied.

"Shut up, nigga. Here go the keys, here the dealer's name and number if you ever need to call him after we done, and on the back is the other number you asked about."

He took the card and flipped it over to read the back. The name, Carlos, was written in ink with a phone number under it.

"How the hell you get his number that quick?" he asked curiously.

"I told you my girl used to fuck with him too. He ain't hard to find if you know the right people."

"Damn, that's love. I really needed to catch up with him."

"Anything for you, big daddy," she teased like always. Bones always thought her voice was sexy as hell.

He finished rolling up the weed and passed it to her.

She lit the blunt, took a seat on the leather sofa next to Bones, and crossed her legs.

"I'ma keep it real," she started. "I know why you wanted Carlos' number, that's why I made sure you had it. I heard that nigga is on that tip, and I think he would be a good addition to your team." She took another hit and exhaled as she continued with sincerity. "I don't expect you to tell me all your business, 'cause trust me, I don't even wanna know. But whatever I can do to help, just let me know. I didn't hold you down all this time to turn my back on you when you got out. So... just let me know if you need me."

He let her words sink in as they floated the weed back and forth. He knew Oshiwa was exactly the kind of girl he needed around at that time, and he also remembered the conversation he had with Skip about her. On the other hand, he knew she had grown accustomed to a certain lifestyle, and she could still have an agenda. Bones wanted to question her about her motivation, but after all the love and loyalty she had shown since his brother's death, it wasn't a conversation he felt that he needed to have.

"I'ma extend the same offer to you, baby. If you need me for anything, I'm one phone call away. I ain't the type of nigga to ever forget when somebody was in my corner, so if I got it, you got it, feel me?"

"That's good to know," she said.

They began to reminisce about Dontae and shared a few laughs thinking about his ways and all the good times they had shared. Oshiwa had been around for as long as Bones could remember, and it wasn't surprising that when Dontae came back home, he ran back to her.

"You know, you remind me of him in some ways, even though y'all don't look shit alike. Just the real nigga shit y'all be on. It's rare now days."

"Shit, who you telling?"

"I know you know. But with you coming back, I just feel like I have a piece of him with me again, and it feels good."

Bones didn't really know what to say. He knew she had a lot of love for him, but for a minute there, it was almost starting to feel like something else.

"Did you ever get the tattoo with his name?" he asked.

"Yeah, I got it right after I told you I was gonna do it. It's right here," she said, standing and turning to reveal a small tattoo on her left calf the read RIP Dontae.

"Nice."

"Did you get any tats in jail?"

"Yeah, I got one on my back."

"What is it?"

"It's a skull and crossbones with my name over it. It's gangsta."

"Well, let me see it."

Bones stood up and pulled the white T shirt he was wearing over his head and turned his back to her. He could feel her hands gliding across the tattooed parts of his body. Then her hands went from his back to his stomach and then his chest. Bones didn't say anything. He had done too much time to be morally concerned about what would happen next. He had heard Oshiwa was amazing in bed, and now he wanted to find out for himself. He turned around and looked down into her eyes. As they shared an intense stare, he reached out and palmed her ass with both hands.

"You sure this what you want?" he asked.

"Been waiting for it a long time," she said as she pulled him by the belt back to the sofa and nudged him back down on it. She unzipped his jeans and took out his rod. The length and width of it was impressive.

"Ummmm," she moaned as she took it into her warm inviting mouth.

The sensations gave Bones the biggest erection he'd had in years, and he couldn't do anything but throw his head back, close his eyes, and enjoy the skilled head master at work. She gave him all tongue and lip service with no teeth in the vicinity. Her jaws were tight like a virgin pussy and wet like a juicy apple. Just as he was about to cum, she eased his dick out of her mouth and began to undress.

Bones stood up and lowered his pants and boxers as she climbed on all fours on top of the sofa. Her body was a flawless brown masterpiece of art.

"Now come and kill this pussy," she ordered, exciting Bones more than he wanted her to know.

He dug inside of her, unprotected and overzealous. She was super tight; it was obvious she had been saving herself for a minute. Their cries of passion rang throughout the house as he tickled her guts, giving all of him that she could stand. He pinned her head down on the couch as he felt the rush coming through his body for the second time. She wasn't going to stop this nut, he was going to release all of it right inside her.

He grunted as the explosion shook both of them. She screamed in ecstasy right before he collapsed on top of her breathing heavily. This was just the pussy Bones needed to feel like he was officially a free man again.

CHAPTER 6

Heaven on Earth was a popular restaurant in Downtown Detroit that served a wide variety of food. It was also Michelle and Leslie's go to spot. They had an elegant table for two in the middle of the restaurant, which made Michelle easily recognizable as her table was so exposed to everyone coming and going. She was quickly becoming a familiar face in the city, but she didn't consider herself a celebrity. It was such a humbling situation whenever someone actually asked for her autograph. She ordered filet mignon and a Caesar salad along with a diet coke.

"Now, all we gotta do is work on getting you a man," Leslie teased.

"You paying for your own lunch, slut, I'm tired of you already."

"I'm just saying. It's been about nine or ten months since you stopped dating ole boy that shall remain nameless. Don't you think it's time to get back in the race?"

"Guys play too many games. I just don't need the distraction right now," Michelle said.

As if on cue, they noticed three handsome well-dressed men enter the restaurant. They were quickly seated up front close to the bar.

"Besides," Michelle continued, "nobody ever asks me out except for guys I work with, and you know my rule on that."

"Nobody else asks you out because you never go anywhere. Home, work, work home. This is the first time you even hung out with me in months. How you gonna find a man like that?"

"I'm not looking for one. And when did you become such an expert on the subject of dating? You've been with the same guy for the last six years."

"Exactly, and I know... wait a minute girl," Leslie said, calling her attention to the gentleman approaching them.

"How you ladies doing today?" Jay said. He was dressed in a powder blue short-sleeved Sean John shirt with matching jeans, along with sky blue Maury's gators with a tennis shoe grip.

"Now wait a minute, Mr. Tall Dark and Handsome. Before you go into your mack mode, you should know that this big rock on my finger is to let the world know that I am officially off the market." Leslie blurted out.

"Shut up fool," Michelle giggled.

"Well, I don't have a mack mode. I have a Jason mode that suits me just fine. But I came over because your friend looks familiar. Are you Michelle Mitchell from Channel 6?"

"Yes I am, how are you?" Michelle said as she offered her hand and Jay accepted.

"I'm doing well, how's the food?"

"I love it. This is my spot. We come here all the time."

"Okay, this is my first time eating here. I noticed your accent, are you from the south?"

"North Carolina."

"Yeah, I got family in North Carolina, Roanoke and Charlotte."

"Get out of here! I'm from Roanoke," Michelle said getting excited.

"Uh oh, you bet not be my cousin," Jay said drawing laughter from the women.

"You never know. It's a small world. Do you ever visit?"

"Yeah, yeah, I was there two summers ago. We hung out a little in VA."

"I love VA," Michelle commented.

"Yeah, it was fun. Anyway, I don't wanna take up too much of your time, but... I don't see a ring on your finger. Are you seeing someone?" Jay asked, seizing the opportunity.

Michelle was feeling his confidence, and he was attractive, but she had just finished saying it wasn't the right time to focus on dating.

"I am newly single, but right now I'm just taking a time out for self. But I'm very flattered you would ask."

"I understand," Jay said unfazed. "Just don't take too much time out. Everybody needs a special someone to share life with."

For the life of him, Jay didn't know where the fuck that line came from, but it sounded good so he let it roll. He wanted Michelle's attention badly.

"Is that what you're looking for, Jason? A special someone?" Michelle was still intrigued.

"Most of the time, people don't know what they want until they find it," he stated truthfully. "But I'll leave you my card if that's okay, and you can give me a call if things change."

"That's fine," Michelle agreed, taking his card and saying waving bye with her free hand.

Jay strolled back to the table with Gunner and E. The smell of his cologne lingered in the air after he departed, as Michelle glanced at the Damn Good Music business card. She was lost in the scent, and regretting the state of her personal life when Leslie snapped her back to reality.

"Bitch what is your problem? You just let a perfectly good man get away."

"You don't know a thing about him but his name. And I didn't let him get away, I took his card," she spat.

"Well, I don't need to know nothing about him, you do"

Michelle went back to her food, as did Leslie, but she couldn't help but glance up front to where Jay was seated a couple of times and wonder to herself what he was really like.

After dinner, Michelle drove home listening to Beyonce's first solo album, Dangerously in Love. She tried her best to sound like Beyonce when her favorite track, "Speechless" blared out of the speakers of her black Range Rover. She could hold a note, but she was no Beyonce by far.

When she made it home, she changed from her dress and heels into a jogging suit and running shoes. Nothing could end the night better than a powerful workout session and the 24 hour Bally's. Exercise had been her peace of mind since she was a teenager. She glanced at her cell phone which was plugged into the cigarette lighter, and wondered when was the last time a man had called her, besides her dad? For a split idiot second, she actually thought about calling her ex just to see how he was doing.

"All I need is a good workout," she reminded herself. "Some leg lifts, lunges, crunches, maybe a few sets of squats." She said aloud. She would probably finish with the treadmill and then head home for a nice long bubble bath. That sounded like the perfect plan.

~~~

Jay woke up thinking about the news reporter he ran into at the restaurant the day before. Since then, she had crossed his mind more times than he would have admitted to anyone but himself. She was so beautiful, and had the brightest smile he'd ever seen. Her skin looked so healthy and flawless, but her eyes were the most hypnotizing thing he noticed about her features. Her light brown eyes had a fire inside of them that gave you a first impression about her without even knowing the woman. He'd had more beautiful women than he could count, but Jay saw something so different with her, it was like a light bulb went off in his head. In Michelle, he saw a class act, with substance and ambitions. It was all in her eyes, he thought. What he didn't see in her eyes was any hint of the gold digger syndrome.

As he pulled into Bake's driveway, he looked at the clock and noticed it was almost time for the midday news. He was sure that Michelle would be on there because he had gone back and forth yesterday searching for her on the nightly news with no luck.

Jay rang the doorbell and a woman with large breasts and long weave answered wearing a T-shirt and panties.

She spoke, giving Jay a seductive glance as he entered the house.

He didn't respond, instead he shot past her and began looking for the remote control to the flat screen mounted on the wall. Bake emerged from the kitchen wearing an apron and a chef's hat. Jay could smell the odor of powdered cocaine settled all through the house. Jay couldn't take him serious at the moment. His was focus on finding Channel Six.

"What's up, my nigga?" Bake said.

"What up, I'm trying catch the news right quick, you dig?"

"Why? What happened?"

"Nothing. I wanna see Michelle Mitchell. I always knew she was cold muthafucka, but when you see her in person, oh my God!"

"Where you see her at?"

"Downtown at Heaven on Earth."

"You shoot at her?"

"You know I had to shoot my shot, Shake-n Bake, but she wasn't really talking what I was trying to hear, ya dig?"

"Oh, you remember Precious don't you?" Bake said noticing that she had made herself comfortable in the living room with them.

"Yeah, yeah," was all Jay would offer. "Let me holla at you for a minute."

The two strutted off to the kitchen where there were big cookie rocks of crack drying on several glass and porcelain dishes.

"You sure you trust this bitch to be up in here while you doing all this? Sometimes you can't let a bitch see too much," Jay warned.

"I know you don't really know the bitch, but trust me, Jay, she's a thoroughbred. I been fucking with Precious for years and years."

"Ok, my nigga, if you say so, then that's what it is."

They slapped fives. Jay trusted Bake, and if Bake trusted her, then he had to believe he wasn't thinking with his dick on this one.

"Here go your girl," Precious called out from the living room.

"Aww shit," Jay took off like somebody had yelled the police were coming, just to get in front of the TV and see Michelle. He was mesmerized by her every word as she stood in front of a hospital reporting a story on a flu vaccine that had strong side effects and had caused people to file a lawsuit against the hospital.

"That's a coooold muthafucka," Jay said.

"Damn Jay, you done became obsessed with this bitch overnight?"

"Watch yo mouth, nigga!" Jay teased. "Naw, but for real, I gotta bump back into her."

"You know who could probably get you in contact with her?"

"Who?" Jay asked at full attention.

"That hoe ass nigga, Dawson. You know he be rubbing elbows with all the high society muthafuckas."

"Damn, you right," Jay said as he thought about the mayor's son. Dawson was always talking about who he knew and what they did for him. He was definitely connected; there was no denying that.

Jay still moved whole kilos hand to hand to the people that would only deal with him. After he made a drop off, he called Dawson to meet up with him, using the thousand dollars he owed him as an excuse. Really, he was trying to pry some information out of him about Michelle if he had any.

They met on Lasher and Grand River in front of a Bookstore/coffee shop. Jay pulled up behind Dawson's BMW 745 then got out and walked over to the passenger side. Dawson hit the auto locks and Jay cracked the door open halfway.

"You got anything in the car with you?" he asked cautiously. Better safe than sorry.

"Naw, you good, come on," Dawson said as he took some paperwork from the passenger seat to make room. Dawson was Mahogany brown with curly hair. He dressed and looked the part of a boss, and even had the money to back it up, but somehow Jay just never bought into it.

"Nigga you know you could have just got with me on the next go round. You didn't have to drive all the way across town to give me this little shit."

"Actually, I had something else I wanted to holler at you about too."

"Oh, what's going on?" Dawson said looking nervous.

Jay went in his pocket and pulled out a bankroll of fifties and twenties. He peeled off twenty fifty dollar bills then handed them to Dawson.

"You ever met the reporter that works for the Channel Six news? Her name is Michelle Mitchell?"

"Yeah, I know her. Met her a few times when my pops was campaigning and whatnot."

"Oh okay, so you don't know her that well?" Jay said going fishing.

"No I ain't never fucked her if that's what you asking. I just know she's a classy bitch, you know? And, I know she went to the Olympics back in 2000. I think she won a medal."

"Damn." Jay said, even more impressed than he already was.

"What, you trying to get to know her or something?" Dawson inquired.

"Yeah, something like that."

"Well dig this, playboy, you in luck. It's a fundraiser coming up on Saturday. I already got some extra tickets on deck. It's some community revitalization type of shit, but it's a black tie affair. Channel Six is covering the event, so nine times out of ten Michelle will be there."

"You say Saturday, huh?"

"Yeah, you rolling? All you need is a tux."

Jay didn't have to think it over long. He didn't have anything to lose by showing up at a fund raiser he cared nothing about. He was pretty sure Dawson didn't either.

"Yeah," he said, nodding his head with purpose. "Yeah I'm in that bitch."

CHAPTER 7

J ay and Dawson arrived at the hotel where the fund-raiser for the rebirth of Detroit's Centerline area was being held in a stretch Mercedes Benz limousine. Dawson had a date and his sidekick/bodyguard along with him, while Jay flew solo. They stepped out right in front of the entrance and were immediately greeted by some professionals Dawson knew through his father as they blended into the crowd headed inside.

Dawson rocked a Gucci suit with diamond cufflinks to match his iced out pinky ring. Jay looked suave in his three piece Tom Ford suit and matching loafers. The flooded Presidential Rolex beamed with every twist and turn his arm made. He was a businessman himself, so he quickly became comfortable in the environment populated with entrepreneurs and wealthy politicians.

He moved about with a bold confidence, and tried not to scan the room for Michelle. If she was there, he hoped she would notice him first. After all, he thought he had left a pretty good impression on her. As the time passed, Jay stood with Dawson getting acquainted with some of the most powerful people in the city of Detroit. He met the Mayor, the Chief of Police, and a few members of the NAACP, introducing himself as an entrepreneur who owned a chain of record stores, which was in fact true.

Deciding to break away from his crutch and do a little mingling on his own before dinner, he ran into the Channel Six sports reporter, who he always thought was pretty cool. They were having a great conversation about the future of the Detroit Lions when Jay felt someone tap him on his shoulder. He turned to see a woman wearing a peach high-low gown and gold necklace with a diamond encrusted heart.

"Excuse me, have we met? You look very familiar."

He studied her face then quickly remembered she was with Michelle the day they met at Heaven on Earth."

"I think we met at Heaven or Earth. You were with Michelle Mitchell," he said, getting excited inside as he hung on her next words.

"Oh yes, that's it. What are you doing here?"

"I'm actually here with the Mayor's son," he stated proudly.

"Wow, what a small world. Wait... I don't want to break up your conversation, but I need you to come with me for a second." she insisted.

Jay played it cool as a cucumber as if he didn't know what to expect, but his fingers were crossed as she led him across the ballroom floor where he quickly locked eyes with Michelle Mitchell mingling with her coworkers. She was wearing a turquoise bustier gown that flared out at the bottom, with off white oval earrings and matching pearls. Her spiral curls hung past her shoulders as she tossed her head back in laughter, gripping her clutch purse with both hands. She was so stunning, it almost took Jay off his A game, but then his ego stepped in and took over.

"Look who I found mingling in the crowd," Leslie said with a colossal grin plastered across her face.

"So we meet again," Jay said stepping up to bat.

"Oh yeah, from the restaurant right?" Michelle said smiling and enjoying his presence.

"Yeah, I came out to support, you dig. Anything I can do to help better Detroit, I'm all for it. But you're looking beautiful as always."

"Well thank you, you're not too shabby yourself. Tell me your name again."

"It's Jason, my friends call me Jay."

"Okay, I will remember this time, Jay. Can I call you Jay?"

"Only if that's means we're friends," he shot back with a grin.

"Well… you seem friendly enough," she flirted.

Jay laughed, enjoying every moment. "You know my homeboy, Dawson? The mayor's son?" he asked, trying to make sure Dawson was giving him the whole story.

"Oh yeah, we've met a few times," Michelle cooperated. "He's a friend of yours?"

"I wouldn't say friend."

"What would you say?" she shot back.

"I'd say homeboy again."

"I heard he was a bad boy," Leslie finally commented.

"I wouldn't know. He's always been a perfect gentleman with me," Jay joked, getting a good hardy laugh from the girls."

"Well, you two stay here. I'm gonna work the room a little longer and finish showing off this dress," Leslie said before darting off and leaving the two of them alone.

"You know, I've thought about you a couple times since the day we met at the restaurant."

"Yeah?" Michelle said with a slight grin.

"I heard what you said about needing some time for yourself, and I can respect that. I just wanna make a connection, and hopefully you'll keep me in mind when things are clearer for you."

"Connection?"

"Connection as in line of communication and door that's cracked open instead of shut and locked with the deadbolt on it, you dig?"

"Where did you see a deadbolt now? Don't be dramatic," she teased.

"I'm just saying."

"No, I hear what you saying and… it doesn't sound like the worst idea I've ever heard."

"Wow, that's all I get, huh?" Jay said and chuckled. From the looks of things, she really was going to make him work."

"I don't know. What did you do before you went into the retail record business?" she pried further.

"I've tried a lot of stuff. Real estate, landscaping. Music just seemed to be the easiest and most successful," Jay shot back without hesitation. He could easily give her a totally legit background of his life because he'd always been trying to start up legitimate businesses since the age of twenty one. He knew he if he told her the truth, she'd run for the border, so he kept his life on the streets under the covers for now.

"Well, I'm glad you found your niche," Michelle said as she went back and forth with herself about the man standing in front of her. *Yes, he is attractive, and yeah he could hold my attention in a conversation. But, is this the right time to entertain the thought of someone new?* She kept thinking. *And who the hell walks around saying 'you dig' all the time?*

Waiters moved about with champagne and hors d'oeuvres, which included deviled eggs, oysters, and ham rolls stuffed with blue cheese. Michelle wasn't big on finger food, but she needed something to put in her mouth and chew on while she decided what to do.

"I'll take one of those," she said, going for the deviled eggs before the waiter got too far.

"You want a glass of champagne?" Jay asked as he reached out to grab one for himself.

"No thanks, I don't drink."

"Not even on birthdays?"

Michelle giggled. "Sometimes... I guess it depends on the birthday.

"Well, I'm not too big on drinking myself, but times like this, it seems like a glass of champagne just sets the tone for the night."

Michelle grabbed some grape juice from another waiter, while Jay sipped slowly on his champagne and continued to engage her in conversation that not only kept her interest, but took her mind off her indecisiveness. She told him a little more about herself, and Jay opened up more as well. There was still a dinner to come, and a performance by a local celebrity R&B singer.

When Leslie came back to them, Jay felt he had solidified himself as date worthy, and he was comfortable leaving the ball in her court. He also knew he had a friend in Leslie to help him seal the deal.

"Well... been a pleasure getting a chance to chat with you again. I don't want to seem pushy, so I'm gonna go catch up with my crowd and let you ladies enjoy the rest of your evening," Jay said before turning to make his exit.

"Your card," he heard Michelle say.

"Excuse me?" Jay was not sure what was said.

"I think I misplaced the business card you gave me."

"Well, let's just make sure you have one in your possession before we go our separate ways."

Jay went in his wallet and pulled out a business card then handed it to her for the second time. *She better be worth all this damn trouble*, he thought to himself.

"Thank you, enjoy your night," Michelle said, blushing a little.

Michelle and Leslie stood side but side and remained quiet until Jay was out of ear reach.

"You can thank me later," Leslie finally said.

"Oh shut up," Michelle shot back.

CHAPTER 8

A t the end of the night, Jay was driven back to his east side store location where his car was parked. Gunner and Bake had keys to the building and Gunner had let everyone into the office so they could all do money drops and re-ups if necessary. Everyone was there except Bake. When Jay came in, Gunner and E were engaged in a dice game, with Detroit rap legend, Blade Icewood, playing at low volume on the stereo.

"Damn ,nigga, you look like you just came from the muthafucking Oscars or something," Lines commented as Jay came in.

"Don't get it twisted. I'm still a killa, muthafucka," Jay joked.

As he surveyed the room, he had a strange thought. He wondered which one of his friends would he feel comfortable introducing to a girl like Michelle. Maybe E and Gunner, since she'd already seen them and they could conduct themselves in public for the most part. But Bake? Probably not. J-Rock? No. Lines? Fuck no!

If there was even a hint of him being a hustler, he was sure Michelle would run like water from a busted sink pipe.

"I know where you been." Gunner said, shaking the dice with a smirk. "How did it work out for ya?"

"I don't know yet, dog. She was there and I hit with everything but the muthafucking kitchen sink."

"You set up a date?"

"Naw, she asked for my card again though, so we'll see. Anyway, mind yo business before I call Kelly and tell her you in here gambling."

"Nigga, you know my wife don't run me," Gunner shot back as E shook the dice.

"Right now, you ain't gotta worry about wifey running them pockets, you gotta worry about me," E said right before tossing the dice up against the wall.

"I need some drugs, Jay. Let me get what I gotta get so I can go hit the street," J-Rock said as he tossed Jay a bag full of Money.

"How much is this?" Jay asked.

"That's nineteen, it's all there."

Jay opened the brown paper bag and peeked in, but didn't bother counting it in front of J-Rock. He would count later on before he stashed it in the re-up count.

"Damn J-Rock, you ain't playing no games out here."

"Hell naw, ain't got time to play. Too much money to be made."

Jay was proud to see his little homey catching on to the grind and making his way. It wouldn't be long before he'd be riding foreign and buying property like his counterparts. Jay took the money, stashed it in a temporary hiding spot, and came back with a whole brick of cocaine wrapped in a shopping bag.

"Be careful nigga," Jay said.

"Always. I'm going out the back. Somebody lock the door."

Jay let him out the back door, and when he turned around, Lines was standing there with the stupidest look on his face holding a bag with a drawstring on it.

"I'm a little short, man," Lines said.

"How short?"

"This fifty three," Lines said looking pitiful.

Lines owed Jay fifty-seven thousand dollars for three kilos. He was four grand short. Jay knew why he was doing this. Lines thought that because it was him who made the Cali connection Jay was about to get, he was entitled to a little more than everyone else. He had met the connect on a coke binge out in LA a few months back. He felt that this connect would be a major come up for everyone. In a way, he was right, but Jay felt that he went about it the wrong way. Jay didn't say a word, he just took the cash and went to put it in the temporary hiding spot.

All of a sudden, shots rang out from right outside the store, causing everyone inside to drop to the ground and draw their weapons. After five shots, there was silence. Jay wasn't armed, but as soon as he got to his feet he went to his desk, pulled out the Glock 33 and ran out to check on everybody.

"Man, what the fuck is going on?" Gunner said, steaming mad that someone had enough balls to buss shots that close to their turf.

Lines was already halfway out the back door with his gun in hand. Jay followed close behind him while Gunner and E checked the front entrance. When Jay and Lines got out back, they made their way to the front of the building. From there, they could see J-Rock's jeep had jumped the curb and crashed into the cemetery gate.

"Aww, fuck!" Jay screamed as he and Lines took off running down the street with guns out for the world to see. By the time they reached the main street, they could see E and Gunner jumping in their cars to pull down to what would soon be a crime scene.

Running in loafers, Jay blew past Lines and made it to J-Rock's driver seat. He was hoping J-Rock wasn't inside and had made it out on foot, but when he peeked in, all he saw as his friend stretched out from the driver to the passenger side, slumped over with a hole in the side of his head.

"Is it bad?" Lines asked before he made it to the jeep. He didn't want to look for himself.

"Go get your truck. Tell E to back up and drop you off to your truck. We gotta take him to the hospital."

Thinking on his feet, Jay knew how much damage they could do moving a wounded man, so he wanted to make the transition easy as possible.

E was just pulling up and Lines hopped in the car with him. Gunner was out of his car now, trying to get some type of response from J-Rock.

"J-Rock, if you hear me, baby, just hold on. Fight for your life, my nigga, just hold on. We got you, baby, we got you."

"Fuck man, hurry up!" Jay shouted, waving at E, who was driving as fast as humanly possible.

E drove in reverse back to Lines' truck then followed Lines back to where J-Rock lay bleeding. Lines jumped out, flung the back door open and held it.

"Come on, Jay," Gunner said as Lines looked on.

The two of them attempted to pull J-Rock's limp bloody body from the jeep. Gunner dragged him out by the torso and then Jay grabbed his legs and helped get him into the suburban. There were no signs of life, but Gunner still tried to coach J-Rock to fight.

"E, get that dope out the jeep," Jay said as they stabbed off toward the nearest hospital.

Lines drove at extreme speeds, running every stop sign and red light he came across. J-Rock's body shifted in the backseat as the truck ran over potholes.

"Who did this shit?" Jay said, thinking aloud as they pulled into the Detroit Receiving Hospital emergency entrance.

Lines was first out the truck before it had completely stopped. He ran through the electric doors and into the lobby.

"Aye, can we get some help out here? My friend just got shot."

"Where is he?" a man in hospital whites asked.

"Right out front," Lines responded with panic in his voice.

The man signaled to some people, while Lines explained the situation. Less than minute later, they came back with a stretcher and headed out to the truck.

As Lines and Jay tried to assist the male nurse in getting Lines on the stretcher, Jay became more engrossed in his own thoughts by the second. By now, he had realized that J-Rock was gone. His Tom Ford vest was covered in too much blood. The hole in his head was too big. No one could survive a wound like that.

~~~

"Jay, what the fuck happened?" Niecey Girl shouted as Jay and Gunner walked in covered in blood, with Lines close behind.

"J-Rock got shot," he said as he moved past her and went to the end table and picked up her house phone.

"Oh my God!" she squealed.

As he began to dial a number, he stopped and slammed the phone back down.

"Niecey Girl, can you call his mother? I can't do that shit right now, but she needs to know."

"What do I say? Is he gonna make it? Is he okay?"

"It don't look good. It don't look good at all," Jay confessed.

Just then, there was a knock at the door.

"That's probably Bake and E," Gunner said as they all took a seat in the living room while Jay answered the door.

Bake and E came through the door brandishing AK 47s with doubled up banana clips duct taped together. Niecey Girl didn't say a word. She knew if J-Rock died, it would be a lot of this behavior going on for a while.

"We got a real problem," E said as he set the Chopper on the table and Bake stood his up in the corner with the barrel to the floor.

He went in his back pocket, pulled out a brown paper bag and dumped the contents on the table. It was all kinds of animal bones. Rib bones, chicken bones, fish bones, you name it. "I found this in the car with J-Rock. I thought it was some money or work, that's the only reason I grabbed it. Somebody tossed this in the car with him after they shot him."

"I don't get it," Lines said confused.

"You saying Bones did this?" Gunner quickly assumed.

"Think about it, who we got beef with?" E said.

Jay just sat on the sofa with his head in the palm of his hand. Last thing he'd heard about Bones was that he was serving twelve years for a murder in Ohio. Now, he was somehow still able to reach out and touch a member of his crew? He took a deep breath.

"Niecey Girl, call the hospital and see if you can find out something about J-Rock. Then, call his mother for me. I'll give you the number," Jay said.

"Okay," Niecey Girl said, ready to cooperate with whatever the crew might need from her.

"It don't look good for him, man," Jay repeated.

"So what the fuck we gonna do, Jay?" Gunner asked.

"We need to find out is this nigga, Bones, out of jail, or is he putting money on niggas or something, because that weak shit he just pulled didn't make sense. Why hit J-Rock when he could've laid in the cut and waited for me or you to come walking out of that muthafucka? Now we know he trying to lay a play down, so... you fucked up by exposing your hand like that," Jay analyzed, referring to Bones.

Jay knew this incident would bring the beast mode out of him that he tried so hard to contain for the sake of his own freedom and all the lives that depended on him. *Sometimes, people don't understand nothing but blood,* his father used to say. He never forgot that valuable lesson.

"They won't tell me nothing at the hospital, Jay. You still want me to call his mom?"

Jay gave Niecey Girl the number to J-Rock's mom, and right away, images of J-Rock's body slumped over inside his car flashed in his mind. He closed his eyes and massaged his temple, trying to ward off the oncoming migraine he felt. Death was always a hard pill to swallow when it's someone you love.

Lines and Gunner were both rolling weed at the same time.

"If the nigga is out, we don't even know where to start looking for him," Gunner complained as Jay began to remove some of his bloody clothing.

"Well, if he's out here, we about to sniff his ass out."

CHAPTER 9

Michelle sighed as she sank into the seams of her Capricorn leather lounge. She had slipped into her gown, and now she was doing something she very rarely did. Stretched out on her side with the remote control in her hand, skipping between Seinfeld reruns and the news, she only wanted to see if her suspicions about Andrea Nelson, a nightly news street reporter, were true.

Andrea started work at the station around six months after Michelle. She was a street reporter also. They'd had some conversations here and there, but never became more than cordial at work. In the conversations that they'd had over the years, it was easy to surmise that Andrea and her had a lot of the same goals, were headed and the same direction, and Andrea felt that made her competition. Michelle didn't see it that way, because she honestly believed that what God had for her could never be taken away.

The last couple of times she managed to catch the news, it was because she was going to have to do a follow up on a story Andrea ran the night before. Michelle had her own style of reporting that set her aside from the rest of the reporters at the station. She wasn't the only one with a unique style, but at least she had one. She was beginning to feel that Andrea was somewhat mimicking her style of reporting. The way she liked to use her free hand for effect, gripping her fingers and thumb together, the way she kept the cameraman moving instead of standing still, and the way she over dramatized her dialog in sections. It sounded crazy to her at first, but after she saw it again, it was almost impossible to ignore. This was her final attempt to convince herself that she was possibly wrong about Andrea, and that her ego had just gotten the best of her.

Jumping from Seinfeld, she came back to the news and finally caught Andrea reporting on a murder that happened near Van Dyke and Six Mile. Andrea was already doing it. The free hand thing.

"Witnesses say that someone on a motorcycle pulled up to a stop sign and began firing into the vehicle. This scene was complete chaos only hours ago, but as you can see, the vehicle that crashed into the cemetery gate has been removed."

Andrea moved in half circle, showing the viewers a shot of the cemetery in the background. It was so blatantly obvious now, that she couldn't believe she hadn't seen it sooner. She wondered how long had it been going on. She turned the volume up to tune in on her dialog, and her mouth fell open.

"Oh my God. Is she impersonating me? What the hell?" Michelle exclaimed to the empty room.

She wanted to call Leslie, but it was after eleven o'clock, so she decided it would have to wait. Although she was now concrete solid with confidence in her suspicions, she still had to let some other people see it and process it for themselves before she got herself all worked up about it. To her, it was very big deal. People have made their mark in the fields of journalism and media by standing out in the crowd. This bitch had her feeling like a dime a dozen. She tried to keep herself calm, but inside she was furious.

As the story ended, she thumbed the power button on the television then got up and stormed into her bedroom. She tried her best to never go to bed angry, so she opted to take her mind off it for now so she could go to sleep in peace. Her mind drifted back to the thought that had taken up a lot of her free time that day... Jason. She was seriously considering reaching out to him, but still hadn't weighed all the pros and cons. Calling a guy felt like she was courting instead of being courted. Maybe. She still had to think about it.

As she went over the enjoyable conversation they had at the fundraiser, she realized he had mentioned that one of his record stores was located in the area of the shooting on the east side. She took it as coincidence and nothing more as she wiggled in the bed getting comfy. She decided to get some rest and she would be able to think more clearly tomorrow about everything.

~~~

Bones had Oshiwa traded in his brother's Lexus for newer model and different color; a 2005 black 460 LS. As he pulled up at the new property he and Skip had acquired, he couldn't wait to get all the gritty details of the murder from his hired gun, Carlos. He had decided it was wiser to get in contact with Carlos through his sister, Trina. That way, his interest in Carlos wouldn't raise any antennas. He knew Carlos probably had created some enemies by now, and he wanted to establish himself as ally not the enemy. This would be their second time meeting face to face about the hit.

Bones met Carlos at the still empty house with no blinds or shades on the windows because it was an area neither of them frequented and they didn't want to be seen together.

Ten minutes later, Carlos pulled up in a late model Buick.

Bones stood in the window peeking outside. The car was probably a rental, Bones thought, because the first time they met up it was the same car, but a different color. He let Carlos in through the front door and their voices bounced throughout the empty house as they greeted each other. Carlos was of mixed race and had softer features. He didn't resemble the killer he had come to be.

"Where the champagne at, nigga? You supposed to be celebrating right now," Carlos joked, knowing he had completed another job with deadly precision.

"Not yet, I got a long way to go," Bones shot back as he fired up his first blunt of the morning.

"Yeah? I hope so, 'cause I been unemployed for nice little minute. I need some work."

"Oh, them bitch ass niggas bout to feel me," Bones assured him as he took a seat on two crates stacked on top of each other. "I wish I would've been there to see the whole play go down and seen the look on that sucker ass nigga Jay's face when he heard the news."

Carlos began reenacting the whole murder for Bones, and he ate it all up with a sinister grin on his face, enjoying every moment. Murder was always an uplifting topic for him.

"I tossed the bones in his lap, pulled the lid down on my muthafucking helmet and skirted the fuck off," Carlos finished.

"They gonna stop hanging at the record store now, we gotta catch 'em in the streets."

"Hell yeah they gonna stop hanging out at that muthafucka. They bet not hang out at either one of 'em and let me catch 'em."

Carlos was so money hungry, he was ready and willing to commit his next murder less than twenty four hours after he'd just shot J-Rock. Bones went into his pocket and pulled out a ten thousand dollar stack wrapped in rubber bands tied the long way. He gave it to Carlos as the balance he owed on the twenty thousand dollar hit.

J-Rock was worth more dead than he was alive.

CHAPTER 10

J ay took it the hardest when the call finally came confirming J-Rock's death. The days leading up the funeral were chaotic because everyone was running around trying to locate the people responsible. Jay closed the eastside location, supposedly for remodeling. He didn't want to put anybody in jeopardy while things were so undetermined. He parked his Benz and hopped in a rental car from Avis so he could move about unde-tected. He knew J-Rock's death was in retaliation for something he had done years ago. He felt responsible, although he knew J-Rock was playing in a dirty game along with the rest of them.

Jay and Gunner had goons all over town trying to find out what they could about Bones from Puritan Ave. It was tricky situation trying to draw information from people. Ask the wrong question to the right person about the wrong person and you could easily find yourself starring down the barrel of a gun.

To take his mind off things, if only for minute, Bake suggested he and Jay go fishing. The weather was nice on a mild spring day, and Jay thought it was a good idea since they hadn't done it in a while. They pulled up in Bake's Cadillac at Angel Park and found their favorite spot was wide open. Bake always said it was the 'mouth of the river,' whatever that meant. The atmosphere was extremely peaceful and serene. Seagulls soared through the air, showcasing their wings and God given ability to rise above it all. The sun was magnificent in exhibiting its face to the world.

"I told Gunner to let me know the minute he get some info or whatever," Jay said, his mind still on the situation in the streets.

They set up shop near a maple tree with snacks, lawn chairs, and a six-pack of Bud Light for Bake.

"Shit, we just gotta be patient. Truth gonna come to the light," Bake said.

"It gonna get ugly for whoever is involved in this. Shit couldn't have come at worse time either. Nigga just beat a murder case and trying to get back to business, and now this shit. I ain't think the nigga Bones would ever come back though. My daddy always said, 'dispose of all enemies, or they gonna come back to haunt you,' and he was right."

Playing chess and fishing were two of the few things Jay got to enjoy with his father growing up. Jay's father was a gangster who went by the name BeeBop and lived by the code of the streets. After he realized his son was a natural born hustler, he began to give him the game as he knew it, furnishing him with all he would need to last in the cold-blooded streets of Detroit and every other hood around the nation.

Jay understood the laws that had to be applied to the streets in order to be successful, as well as the laws that had to be applied in any walk of life to make your way in America. Money and fear were powerful, a happy team is a competent team, and women could be the key to success or failure at any given moment. These were just three of the many jewels that were embedded in Jay's head at an early age.

When Jay was twenty-two, his mother died of cancer only few years before his father would pass away from heart failure while serving a life sentence on a federal conspiracy charge. Being from a small family, all he had now was Niecey Girl and some uppity cousins he chose not to deal with. Van Dyke Down was his family, and he was godfather to Gunner's first born and one of E's children.

Jay continued to vent, just as he had done on the ride all the way there, and Bake just listened, not really wanting to add fuel to the fire. This trip was supposed to take their minds off things for a minute, but Jay was making it hard. Finally, he decided to speak his mind, hoping Jay would see things the same way.

"Listen, my nigga, when we find out what's going on, we gonna do what we gotta do. This the life we chose, you feel me? I know ain't none of us see this shit coming, but... we ain't helping J-Rock by beating ourselves up over this shit."

"You right." Jay agreed.

"We still here and we gotta live, Jay. That's why you don't ever see me stressing about shit, dog, I know we only here for a little while anyway. We gonna get at them bitch ass niggas, but... you know, life goes on."

Jay respected and valued Bake's opinion enough to take it at face value. He agreed that although losing a loved one was the worst thing that could happen to a person mentally, it also made sense that they didn't let the loss consume them. It would surely lead to bad decisions, and Jay had come way too far to slip up again.

"You right, nigga. Let's catch some fish. And you can finish telling me about your pipe dreams of opening up a strip club," Jay joked, trying to adjust his somber mood.

As the day went on, they began to get a little luck on the river, and Bake and Jay both caught a few fish. Bake caught two Pickles and a Catfish, and he was super excited about the Catfish. Jay caught three Pickles. On the ride home, both Bake and Jay rode with their guns in their lap. They were in Bake's car, which was known to everyone, but they stayed cautious, knowing anyone in the crew could be a target.

When they reached Bake's house, instead of tucking his gun under his Polo fleece, Jay kept it in his hand as he transferred all of his belongings from Bake's car to his rental. The two said their goodbyes and Jay went on his way. He had plans to make stops at the other store locations, but for his safety, Gunner would have a couple goons arrive first to watch his back. Everyone understood that not only was Jay the target, he was also the most valuable piece of their puzzle.

His business line rang with an unknown number as he got into the car. He frequently received calls from unknown numbers on the business line, so he answered without hesitation.

"Hello Jason, this is Michelle. How are you?"

"I'm okay, how are you?" Jay answered, still thinking it was a business call.

"I'm fine, thanks for asking."

"What can I do for you today?" Jay asked, thinking someone wanted to confirm some orders or arrival times.

"Excuse me?" Michelle asked realizing she didn't give him enough information. She was already feeling a little jittery, and he wasn't helping. "This is Michelle Mitchell, we met at the—"

"Oh wait, you did say Michelle, didn't you? I'm sorry, it didn't register until now."

Jay's spirit lifted at the sound of her voice. For a split second, he forgot about all his current troubles.

"I'm glad you remember me. I was second guessing myself until I dialed your number," she admitted.

"Really? Why is that?"

"Calling feels like courting," she explained. Three days had passed since the fundraiser, and Jay was still heavy on Michelle's mind.

"Well, I think I not only initiated our connection, I followed it up with a second introduction."

"You can't take credit for that. That was all Leslie," she teased. If only she knew how calculated Jay had been.

"I guess you got a point. So how was your day?"

"Hectic. I had to do a story on a plane crashing at the city airport during an air show, with like, no time to prepare at all."

"Did he die?"

"No, he's gonna live. It was just a big explosion after he crashed. I was trying to get there while the fire was still blazing, but I didn't arrive until an hour after it was out."

"Damn, how'd that happen?"

"Long story, somebody else's screw up that I ended up paying for, but I managed to pull it off without make a mockery of the station."

"Hmmph, the city airport is in my old neighborhood. I used to watch those air shows from my front porch as a kid."

"Really? How cool."

"It was cool."

"That reminds me. Did you know the young guy that was shot and killed near the cemetery on McNichols and Van Dyke a few nights ago?"

Jay was completely flustered and caught off guard by the question. For a moment, he didn't know how to answer it. *But losing a friend isn't something to hide,* he thought.

"Yeah, actually I did know him. I knew him well."

"Oh wow, I'm sorry for your loss."

"Thanks," was all Jay would offer. He wouldn't go into any other detail about J-Rock, and for a moment, the conversation fell silent.

Michelle didn't know what else to say, and Jay wasn't saying anything, so she prepared to end the conversation quickly. "Well, I was just reaching out to touch bases with you and see how your day was going."

"Thanks, I appreciate that," Jay said. His mind had drifted back to J-Rock, and he was no longer a part of the conversation.

Michelle rode out the long pause, expecting some clue that he was actually interested in hearing from her again, but she got nothing.

"Okay, well nice chatting with you. Talk to you later."

"Okay."

As soon as Jay hung up the phone, he realized how he must have sounded to her. It was amazingly bad timing that he had met her right before J-Rock's death. It was also compounded by the fact that she was a news reporter and actually knew about the whole incident. He almost ran a red light as he battled with himself in his mind. The words his friend, Bake, had spoken earlier that day came back to him. *We ain't helping J-Rock by beating ourselves up over this shit. We still here and we gotta live, Jay.*

He knew Michelle was the kind of woman you don't let slip away, hoping you'd run into another like her one day. She was someone who would be healthy for his overall state of mind, especially now. But the timing was ridiculously wrong. He decided to say fuck the time, and he called her back. She quickly answered.

"Hello?"

"Hey, Michelle. Listen, I had a few things on my mind when you called, but I'm not letting you get away that easily. I would love to have dinner with you one day soon if you're free. Again, I know you're not looking for nothing serious right now, but like I said, I'd love to just have dinner."

"I like the sound of that. Can we go to my favorite spot?"

"Heaven on Earth? Wherever you show up at will be heaven for me," he said, pouring it on thick. He could hear the smile in her voice and she flirted back.

"I guess you in your game running mode now."

"I thought I told you before, I only have a Jason mode."

"Ok, Jason, I'm free Saturday if you are, Mr. Smooth."

"I wouldn't miss it for game seven of the NBA finals," he lied.

"Okay, now you just went too far," she teased about the falsehood.

"Okay, you got me, but I'm really, really looking forward to seeing you again, so I'm gonna let you go before you change your mind."

"Okay," she giggled. "Bye Jason."

"Later."

~~~

Saturday morning was the funeral services for J-Rock. Jay hadn't thought about the funeral when he accepted the date with Michelle, but he decided not to cancel, knowing he may not get a second chance. The funeral was held outside of the city and only close friends and family members were invited. Jay paid for all the funeral costs from the nineteen thousand J-Rock handed him right before he died, and gave his family what was left of it.

The whole crew attended the service and drove to the burial site afterwards to see the casket lowered into the ground. A wave of guilt came over Jay as he found himself continuously thinking about Michelle and his date with her later that evening.

The crew met up at Niecey Girl's house after the burial, where she had fried enough chicken for everybody to eat, along with a big pot of spaghetti. They discussed all the latest findings amongst each other, not excluding anything from Niecey Girl's ears. She was just as much a member of their circle as anyone else in the room. Gunner, through the work of his top goons, had been able to confirm that Bones was in fact out of jail and making moves to open drug houses around his old stomping grounds. They came up on the name, Skip, which Jay and Gunner were both familiar with, but had forgotten about. It was a small amount of information, but it was reliable, and it was definitely better than nothing.

"Right now, we just gotta keep the team strong and on point. Nobody else get caught slipping out here, we gotta watch each other's back, ya dig?"

"Nigga, Ray Ray and my young guns on the prowl, nigga. They ready for this shit, watch what I tell you," Gunner assured everyone. He had the deadliest crew of youngsters he'd ever seen on his side, and that was the main reason he kept them around. Just for times like these.

King Benjamin's Perspective:

First off, I don't like this nigga, Bones. He fucking his deceased brother's girl? Foul as hell! Kinda curious about

Ray Ray and these young cats, and why they're being spoken of with such high regard. I mean, if they that bad, seems like they should be in the room strategizing with the rest of the clique. I don't know, maybe it's a Van Dyke thing. And, I don't know if Jay should be focused on the Michelle chick right now, but we'll see. Carry on.

CHAPTER 11

Michelle didn't know enough about Jay to let him come to her house yet, so she definitely made plans to meet him at the restaurant that evening. She pulled up and valeted her Range Rover, feeling a little nervous, but confident that she looked amazing in her knee length black sleeveless Givenchy dress. It was low cut and the custom designed a choker complimented her skin and her cleavage. The sleek texture of her shoulder length tresses, which were parted in the center, shined like the sun. She sashayed in after getting her ticket, and Jay was waiting for her at the door. He looked good. He looked really, really good. His taper and goatee were extra crispy, and he wore a short-sleeved tan button down, matching shorts, and tan Cole

Haans. The Rolex was downright blinding as the diamonds shimmered off the ceiling lighting.

"Hey, Mr. Smooth," she greeted.

"Hey, I know you. You the lady from the six o'clock news," he teased

"Oh my God, don't play. I hope nobody recognizes me today. I'll do just fine to come have dinner in peace and quiet."

"You look amazing." He complimented with his eyes roaming joyfully.

"Thank you. Funny, I was just thinking you don't look bad yourself."

Jay had a table reserved in the rear, and as the hostess came to escort them, he allowed her to walk ahead of him, mostly to get a look at her backside. Boy was he glad he did. It was plump and healthy like fresh fruit straight off the farm. The other reason he wanted her to walk ahead of him was so he could see her reaction when they arrived at the table. Jay had arranged for ten-inch white candles set in sterling silver to be placed on the table and lit upon their arrival. There was also a single white rose wrapped in a card on the table in front of Michelle's seat. As they arrived at the table, the grin smeared across her face told him that as expected, it went over well.

"You think you're slick, don't you?" she asked in an accusing tone as he pulled her chair out.

"What I do?"

"Mmm hmm. I see I'm gonna have to keep both eyes on you."

"I'm just trying to make a good first impression, you dig?"

"Ha, so far so good, ya dig?" she mocked, taking the card in one hand and the flower in the other. The card was very short and simple. It read, *To new friends.* On the inside were two champagne glasses raised in toast. She closed the card smiling.

"This was really sweet. Take me, I'm yours," she teased making Jay laugh hard.

"Seriously though, does it bother you to get noticed a lot while you out in public?

"I mean, yes and no. I took the job knowing what all it entails, right? So, I love being a reporter, and that comes with it, but sometimes it's just like... not today, you know?

"Yeah, I feel that."

"I mean, I'm a very friendly person by nature, so most of the time I'm okay with people just walking up to me and starting a conversation because they know who I am. But sometimes I'm on the move, and it's like, 'can we take a picture?' and I don't always have time, so that's when it gets a little frustrating because I don't want people thinking I'm mean."

Jay listened attentively while getting lost in the beauty of her eyes at the same time. He hoped like hell they were contacts because it would ruin some the mystic energy that was building inside him. From everything his mind had been able to grasp, Michelle was a street nigga's dream. Still, he never felt comfortable with hiding who he was.

Michelle ordered the Mediterranean style Orange Roughy, and Jay the Steak Marinade. The conversation flowed effortlessly as they waited for their food to arrive. Michelle told him about her years as a college gymnast and a little about her current work.

"So why don't you have a Mrs. Smooth?"

"Can you stop with that?"

"Okay, that was my last one. Sooo?"

"This might sound like a bunch of bullshit coming from somebody you labeled Mr. Smooth, but truthfully, I haven't found anyone who was that compatible with me since high school. I mean, I've had some really close friends here and there, but... it seems like the closer you get to people, feelings change. Sometimes it's me, sometimes it's them."

Michelle could definitely relate to what he was saying, so she didn't judge him. She too had come close to knowing love on occasions, only to find it was lust masquerading as someone else.

"How about you? When was your last relationship?" Jay inquired.

"Almost a year ago. Wanna know what caused the break up?" she offered.

"Yeah."

"This is always a fun story to tell. The President of Network News offered to double my salary and make me lead anchor on the evening news, but there was just one small catch. I had to sleep with him, of course. Being the fragile coward that he is, the general manger didn't have the guts to make such a suggestion to my face, so guess who he sent to propose the deal? You got it, my loving boyfriend and coworker of two years."

"Dirty muthafucka," Jay fumed.

"I know right. It got so uncomfortable for us to be around each other after that, he eventually left the station."

"He need his ass whooped, and I'm volunteering," Jay joked.

Michelle giggled and felt herself becoming more comfortable with Jay every minute she was around him. There was something about his charming ways that was magnetic. He was smooth but he was rough, and it was a big turn on. He was an independent man and seemed to be even a little romantic. *Probably too good to be true, knowing my luck,* she thought.

The food came and it was delightful as always, but Michelle enjoyed the conversations that took place between bites even more. Their connection was undeniable.

Two hours later, they realized it was getting late and decided to call it a night. Jay walked her out and stood with her as she waited for the valet to pull her car around. As the cool night breeze flowed around them, Jay stood looking down into her sparkling eyes one last time.

"Tonight was everything I thought it would be," he admitted.

"I had a great time. I'm glad we met, Mr —"

"See, look at you," he said, pointing a finger.

"I didn't say it," she chuckled.

As the black Range Rover pulled up, Jay reached for a hug and Michelle fell into his arms without hesitation.

"I'll be stalking, I mean calling tomorrow," he said.

"I carry a stun gun, and I'm not afraid to use it."

Michelle climbed in her truck and Jay watched her drive away while he waited for valet to bring his car around. Up to this point, Jay had lived a pretty good life for a man under thirty years old. But if he could have just this one lady in his life, it would be the icing on the cake.

As Michelle drove off, she gazed in her side view mirror at Jay in front of the restaurant, while also trying to watch the road in front of her. There was something about this that just felt so right. She wasn't getting her hopes up high, but she wasn't going to be indecisive either. She was open to whatever opportunities lay ahead for her and Jason, AKA Mr. Smooth.

~~~

Once Bones made it to Detroit, he never once thought about going back to Ohio or contacting his parole officer. He got fake ID through his old contacts and went on the run, not giving a fuck about the pending warrant. He and Oshiwa had become almost inseparable as he quickly realized just how much of a valuable asset she would be. He wouldn't have to find someone new to meet the needs of a man in his position, because without even knowing it, he had already secured the perfect ride or die bitch.

Bones didn't bring Oshiwa around family members, knowing the relationship would be frowned upon, but they roamed the Westside of the city day and night with no shame.

Having so much coke to distribute, Bones and Skip quickly established a strong hold on their neighborhood, and it put them in a position to recruit new soldiers. The plans were to spread their wings over the summer and expand into a few more areas, but before that happened, he had to take care of potential threats that would always be lurking. The Van Dyke Down crew had to go, no if ands and buts about it.

He and Oshiwa pulled up to the drug house Bones and Skip had met up at on his first day back in the D. He had a paper tag in the window ready to stunt on Skip, but it was mostly motivation for the young workers they were gathering to do their dirty work.

"Show these little niggas the money and watch how high they jump for you," he said to Oshiwa.

"Exactly," she agreed, sitting comfy in the passenger seat.

The young hustlers filed out of the house and on to the porch with the bright eyed look of admiration in all their eyes. They knew Bones was living the dream they could only aspire to live for the moment.

"You see this young fat muthafucka right here?" Bones said, pointing to kid he now knew as Big Baby.

"Yeah, what about him?"

"I seen Skip beat that nigga like a slave my first day back home. When I pulled up right here, he had him outside on the porch stomping a mud hole in his ass. I'm talking about a beating you get when somebody really wanted to kill you, but chose not to. And guess what it was all about?"

"What?"

"Four hundred dollars," Bones chuckled.

"Damn! Li'l nigga must be a fool for pain 'cause he sure ain't went nowhere."

"Hell naw he ain't went nowhere. Skip made him work it off. He wasn't going nowhere even if he wanted to."

Just then, Skip bent the corner flexing hard in brand new four door Saab. His tag was still in the window too. He hadn't told Bones, but as soon as he found out Bones was going to get something new, he went on a search to upgrade himself.

"Look at Skip hoe ass," Bones said grinning.

"Ha! I guess he said, 'you ain't about to stunt on me nigga,' " Oshiwa commented.

Skip pulled up on the side of Bones and parked in the middle of the street. He jumped out excited and ready to talk some shit.

"Yeah nigga. Fuck you thought? Huh? You thought you was the only nigga going car shopping today? Nigga we getting money out here, this shit ain't no game."

Bones and skip slapped fives while laughing hard going back and forth with each other. It was a moment Bones had waited for years to make happen. The youngsters sat on the front porch idolizing the OGs, and dreaming of the day when their time would come.

"Guess what though, nigga? See me tomorrow and watch me blow your muthafucking wig back."

"What?" Skip said scowling. "What you gone do tomorrow? Huh?"

"Don't worry about it, nigga, see me tomorrow."

"What? Nigga fuck that, see me in a hour nigga."

"Fuck outta here."

"Aye, but fo'real though, you pick up any money from them niggas yet?" Skip asked getting serious.

"Not yet. What, you hurting now you done bought the Saab? You need a loan, nigga?"

"Fuck outta here," Skip said, waving him off. "Oh on some real shit though. I got good news."

"Yeah?"

"Hell yeah. I been busy on them Van Dyke boys."

Bones' face showed that his curiosity had been piqued.

"I'ma drop her off and come back," Bones assured.

"Aiight, do that."

"Where you gone be?" Bones asked as he climbed back into his vehicle.

"Just call me. 'Cause right now I'm bout to go stunting on these hoes."

He mashed the gas and skidded off quickly before Bones could respond.

CHAPTER 12

It was the day of the annual photo shoot for the Channel Six news team. Everyone would be there since participation was mandatory. There would be photos of the reporters taken as a team and then solo shots. The lead anchors would take team photos and then the whole staff including control room personnel and scene technicians would take a group photo. The shoot had to happen quickly because half of the people there had to leave the photo shoot and head straight back to work.

When Michelle arrived on the set, she was feeling fabulous rocking a navy blue business suit and a pair a two carat diamond studs. All week, she and Jay had been chatting and revealing more and more about themselves through long nightly conversations right before her bedtime. She found Jay to be charismatic and intriguing. He was also a little hood, which was something she wasn't used to. It was turn on. He always put her to bed in a good mood, and she usually woke up the next morning felling amazing.

The first person Michelle spotted was Andrea Nelson schmoozing with the general manager and laughing harder than necessary at his jokes.

"Hey Michelle," Kurt, the general manager called out, waving her over.

As Michelle approached, the smile on Andrea's face seemed to slowly evaporate. Andrea was tall, brown and flat chested. She gave Michelle a once over with a bit of contempt in her eyes.

"Hey Michelle, we're so glad you could make it," Andrea said, beating Kurt to the punch.

"Hi Andrea, hello Kurt, how are you?" Michelle said addressing Kurt while dissecting Andrea's strange behavior. She was making it sound as if she had something to do with planning the annual photo shoot, when in reality, Andrea and Michelle had the same exact job titles.

"I'm great, thanks for asking," Kurt replied.

"We missed you at the fund raiser," Michelle informed Kurt.

"Oh, yeah, I was a bit under the weather," Kurt confessed.

"Yes, that's what I heard. But it was an amazing turn-out."

"Yes, it most certainly was," Andrea cut in. "Michelle did you get a chance to meet my husband?"

"Uuh no, I don't think so. I only remember us talking briefly."

"There's my girl! Come here you," a familiar voice called and Michelle turned to see the news director heading straight for her with the biggest grin on his face and his arms extended for a hug.

Michelle and Jim embraced briefly. Jim was a great guy, and Michelle knew he had a thing for her, but he always kept things professional and she respected him for that. From the corner of her eye, Michelle could see the hint of jealousy forming on Andrea's face. Everyone loved Michelle from the day she joined the news team, but Andrea not so much. People tended to view her as a phony ass kisser. As everyone mingled, waiting for the photographers to set up, Andrea seemed desperate for attention. She scurried around forcing interaction on people she barely knew, trying her best to seem relevant. The harder she tried, the more people were turned off by her. By the time she and Michelle got ready to do solitary shots, Michelle could see the beads of sweat forming on her forehead out of frustration. Michelle couldn't help but wonder what was her issue. As the team gathered for the group photo, the news director whispered something to Michelle.

"You heard the news?" he asked.

"No. What news?"

"Diane's leaving in a few months. That means they're gonna be looking for a new anchor woman to take her spot." His eyebrows went up and down as he nodded in Michelle's direction, as if to say, *here's your chance.*

"Really?" Michelle said. It was definitely exciting news.

Is this why Andrea's running around in ass kissing panic mode? She thought. Michelle could not lie to herself –if Diane was leaving, she really wanted this job. Diane was the lead anchor on the evening news. A six-figure salary plus a prime time slot for all her ideas on how to bring change to the station and the Detroit community as a whole. It was truly her dream job, but she wasn't about to get her hopes up, knowing there was a lot of politics involved in picking the lead anchors. For one, Diane was white and her co-anchor was a black man. That fact alone had her thinking in her mind that Diane would more than likely be replaced with another white female. As they all squeezed in for the final shot, Michelle couldn't help but fantasize about how grand her life could become in the very near future.

~~~

"Look, nigga, you gotta stop turning your fucking phone off all the time. Niggas need to know where you at in case something go down," Jay ordered Lines as he slid in the passenger seat and strapped on his seatbelt.

"I know, man. This J-Rock shit just been fucking with me heavy, dog. I was high as a kite last night," Lines confessed, picking at his nose. It was something he did frequently because the cocaine was destroying his nostrils from the inside.

Today was the day that Lines would take Jay to meet up with the connect in southwest. The crew was just about out of drugs, and although J-Rock's death still had everyone on guard, life had to go on. The only solid information they had about Bones was the fact that he was definitely out of jail. Niecey Girl had pulled up his name on the internet and found out his release date. As Jay and Lines rode to southwest, Jay tried to talk Lines into thinking and acting more responsibly, but it only turned into an argument.

"Niggas been looking for you for damn near two days, Lines. The fuck, man? You don't call nobody back, you still driving around in that truck that everybody know. You think this shit is a game, nigga?"

"Man, fuck you, Jay! I did leave you a message on your voicemail letting you know I was straight. Ain't nobody else sitting at home hiding under the covers, so what you want me to do? You still hanging out with the li'l bitch you just met at the fundraiser, Gunner still hanging out, E and Bake still doing them…What the fuck, Jay?"

"Niggas ain't still riding around in them same cars either. As soon as I told them niggas to put them cars up, they switched up. Niggas is checking in on each other every day too, while you still playing stupid like you don't know what's going on. But if you don't appreciate niggas trying to look out for your punk ass, then fuck you too. I'm not into keeping tabs on niggas 'cause I ain't got no kids."

"Okay, Daddy. I went to the club last night. I got in with my banger. I took Ray Ray with me, and he got in with his banger too. I met a bitch, took the bitch to the room, and fucked the bitch. Is it anything else you wanna know about last night?" Line asked sarcastically.

"Yeah okay."

"Huh? You wanna know what the pussy taste like, nigga?"

"Your nasty ass probably did eat her pussy too."

As they arrived in southwest, Jay thought the area always reminded him of Los Angles. Southwest was predominantly a Mexican community, and it was evident in everything from the restaurants to the names of the businesses up and down Junction Street. Jay tried to calm himself as he came closer to their destination. Deep down, he felt like Lines was using J-Rocks death as an excuse to let his coke habit spiral out of control and act irresponsibly. He glanced over at Lines picking at his nose, and was slightly disgusted.

"This spot right here, Jay," Lines said, pointing to a collision shop that had been painted with elaborate graffiti of old school muscle cars. A few esès stood out front politicking in a huddle. Lines called Hector to let him know they were out front.

"Amigo?" Hector answered.

"What's up, baby? I'm outside."

"Okay. Pull around back, my brother's gonna let you in."

They pulled around back of the building. All three shutters were up, and there was clearly work going on inside. It looked as if the collision shop wasn't just a front for moving drugs. As Jay removed the duffle bags from the trunk, he glanced around wisely. A Mexican man of average height appeared in the doorway and waved them in.

As Jay walked in, a strong whiff of car paint smacked him in the face. Latino rap music could be heard on low volume near the work area. The man quickly escorted them to Hector's office. At first glance, Jay's thoughts were that Hector did not look like what he expected. A small baby faced man, he wore his hair in one long braid down the small of his back. He wore a wife beater and no tattoos, which was really odd in Jay's mind.

"Hector, this is Jay, Jay this is Hector," Lines said, making the formal introduction.

"Good to finally meet you, amigo," Hector said.

"Likewise, ya dig," Jay returned as he squared his shoulders ready to get straight to business.

The door to Hector's office had a window that was covered with white blinds. Hector moved from his recliner and pulled down the blinds so no one could peek inside. He could see Jay wanted to get right to business, and so did he. From the cabinet above, he pulled out a money counter and set it on his desk. There was a three foot long chest on the floor behind Hector's desk. He opened the chest with a key and pushed the lid back, revealing keys of cocaine stacked to the top.

"Let's do this," Hector said.

CHAPTER 13

J ay secured twenty bricks at sixteen-five a piece. He
put it out to the crew at eighteen-five each, giving
him a profit of forty grand each flip. With a profit
margin like that, Jay knew he would be a millionaire in
no time. He got everyone set up with their packages, and
then he showered and changed at Niecey Girl's house
where he always kept plenty of clothes. He had a date
with Michelle, and it had been on heavy on his mind
since he left Hector.

Earlier in the week, Michelle had mentioned a play
that was coming to town with some local celebrities and
some b list actors. Whether she was giving Jay a subtle
hint or not, he decided to surprise her the next day with
two tickets to the show. This would be their third date,
and Jay was happy he had earned enough trust to pick

her up from her downtown loft. He picked her up in a 2005 rented Camaro.

~~~

Michelle had given it some thought before she decided to let Jay pick her up from home. She was growing more comfortable with him by the day, and being that the play was right down the street at the Fox Theater; it seemed to only make sense. It was mid-afternoon and the light drizzle that started outside was enough for her to bring an umbrella, but not enough to make the sun cower from the sky just yet. She noticed the car was different than the one he'd driven on their last date. It seemed he was in something different every time.

"Do you also own a car lot Jason?" She asked, siding into the passenger seat.

"Ha. No I don't."

"Well, how many cars do you have, if I can pry?"

"Well, I only own a Mercedes and a truck. I've been driving rental cars since my Mercedes has been in the shop," he lied.

"Did you crash it?" she asked.

"No. A friend did."

"Some friend."

"Never again," he countered with a fake laugh. Jay hated every time he had to lie to Michelle, and he began to wonder was it even worth all the trouble. It was definitely something he knew he couldn't get used to.

They pulled up in front of the Fox Theater and the valet attendant opened the door for Michelle. She could tell he recognized her but wasn't sure if it was her. Inside, she held Jay's hand – not to be romantic, but to make sure they stayed connected as they moved through the jam-packed lobby. They found the usher, who showed them to their seats right before the play started. The play was definitely better than Jay expected. He thought it was something nice to do for Michelle, but was surprised to find himself into it too. The comedic timing was on point, and he and Michelle laughed or didn't laugh at the same things. One thing he had noticed in the past few weeks was they had a similar sense of humor.

Near the end of the show, Jay's cell phone began to ring nonstop. He saw it was Neicey Girl, so after the third call, he stepped out into the hallway to return her call.

"What's up, cousin?"

"Come and get your muthafucking boy!" She yelled in his ear.

"Who?"

"Lines stupid ass!"

"What's wrong? What he do?"

"I don't know what this nigga is on, but he said he hasn't been to sleep in three days, and he is straight tripping. I told him to go lay down in your bed, but this muthafucka went outside and on my porch and just started shooting in the air for no reason. He just flipped the fuck—"

"I'm on my way."

"Okay, but he outside now. I put his ass out, 'cause he can't come back up in here acting like that."

"Fuck!"

Jay hung up the phone with fire on his insides. He stormed back into the theatre in a panic, thinking about all the dope and guns at Niecey's house while this fool was outside shooting. He was putting everyone in jeopardy, including Niecey Girl. If the police arrived before he did, he would never forgive Lines.

"I'm sorry, Michelle, but I gotta go. Something is going on with my cousin."

Michelle could see the panic in his eyes and she immediately grabbed her clutch to leave.

"I'm so sorry. Is she gonna be okay?"

"I'm not sure. I just need to get over there fast."

"Okay, let's go."

The two rushed out of the building before the play ended, and as soon as the valet brought the car, Jay went flying down Woodward to drop Michelle off at home.

"You might wanna slow down a little. You know it's swarming with cops around here," Michelle suggested.

Jay didn't say a word, nor did he slow down. When he pulled into her lot, he swung around and dropped her off right in front of her door.

"I'll call you," he said.

"Okay, and be careful," was all she could say. She exited the car, concerned for him and whomever he was running to rescue.

Jay sped off toward the freeway as the rain began to pour down hard.

When Jay arrived on his cousin's block, he spotted Lines' truck with the driver's side door flung open and the music blaring. He glanced around, feeling a small sense of relief that there were no police in sight. He spotted a man stretched out on the front lawn bucking around sporadically as the rain drenched his body from head to toe. The man began to yell for help, and Jay parked and got out in the pouring rain. He tried to get a good look at the man on the ground, but the severe rain blurred his vision. The closer he got to the man, he could hear him now rapping the words to the song that was playing loudly in Line's truck. Seconds later, it became evident that the crazy man laid out in the grass was his friend Lines. Jay became furious, and as his blood boiled out of control, he was tempted to rear back and kick the shit out of Lines, but he caught himself.

"Lines, what the fuck is wrong with you?" he shouted, snapping Lines out of his cocaine induced escape from reality.

He locked eyes with Jay and grinned, as if he didn't have a care in the world. "I was just washing my clothes, Jay."

"You what?" Jay yelled, ready to punch Lines in the mouth with all his might.

"Get yo ass off my grass!" Niecey yelled from the doorway.

Jay spotted Lines' .40 cal. lying in the grass and picked it up. "Nigga, if you don't get your ass up off this grass, I'ma shoot you myself!" Jay warned.

When Lines saw the pistol, his dilated pupils bucked. He rose from the soaked grass quickly, and wiped the mud from his jeans.

"Naw man, I'm straight, Jay," Lines said still wiping.

"You ain't straight muthafucka, you tripping! You wanna die, nigga?" Jay said clutching the pistol but not pointing it at Lines.

"Whachu mean, Jay?"

"It's a simple question. 'Cause I'll kill you myself before I sit and watch you go out like this."

Lines was standing straight up now, but his posture was slumped and his jaws sagged like a man with a broken spirit.

"Come on, Jay. Put the gun down, man. You can't kill me."

Jay handed him his gun back.

"This your gun, stupid muthafucka."

"I just need some sleep, man. I been up for three days blowing cane, dog. This shit done took over.

Lines looked all of sudden rational, and Jay just wanted to get him away from the house as soon as possible.

"Can you drive?" Jay asked as Lines headed to his truck.

"Yeah dog, I'm straight. Jay, I just need to go to lay down."

"You sure you can drive, man?" Jay asked, not believing he could.

"I'm straight, Jay. I'ma call you tomorrow."

Lines quickly hopped in his truck and pulled off.

Jay still followed him to make sure he went straight home. When he saw Lines pull in his driveway, Jay drove past and kept going. He was still furious at Lines for putting the whole crew at risk. He had ruined his night with Michelle and pissed Niecey Girl off to the point of no return. For the first time ever, he considered cutting ties with Lines altogether.

As Jay drove down Lines' block, he realized he was almost out of gas. He'd have to make a stop at a low-key gas station nearby. Thunder clapped ferociously as the unexpected storm continued to match the mood of the moment.

~~~

Michelle sat at home, hoping everything was all right with Jay. He sounded so upset when they parted; she couldn't help but wonder what had happed and what was going on at that very moment. The curiosity was killing her, and after sitting quietly for too long thinking about it, she decided to undress and try to get comfortable for a night at home alone. She had enjoyed the time they spent together, and deep down she wished it hadn't ended so abruptly. Just then, her cell phone rang and she flipped it open to see that it was Jay calling.

"Hey," she quickly answered.

"Hey. How you doing?"

"I'm good. How are you?"

"I'm good. Everything is good."

"Really? I'm so glad to hear that," she said truthfully.

"You not mad at me for bailing out are you?"

"No, of course not. As long as everything is okay."

"Yeah. My cousin was just having some beef with her boyfriend. She made it sound more serious than it really was."

"Well, good. I'm glad you're okay, and I'm glad she's okay."

"I'm not okay. They fucked up my night!" Jay admitted, causing Michelle to burst into laughter.

"Oh, as if you really had big plans," she teased.

"You know I did," he shot back.

"Yeah, well... they fucked up my night too." Michelle said, shocking herself. It was one of the few times she had let him hear her curse.

"I hope you mean that." Jay said as he drove in search of the best gas station to stop and get gas. He couldn't help but wish he was in route to go and spend time with Michelle.

"It's pretty bad out there, huh?" Michelle said, listening to the constant patter of the rain outside her window.

"Yeah, it's coming down pretty hard." Michelle could hear a conversation in the background. "Give me forty on pump one," Jay told the attendant. He watched his back as he exited the gas station.

"So, what are you doing, Mr. Smooth?"

"Just getting some gas and talking to a pretty girl," he said, moving fast trying to keep from being soaked.

"You mean pretty woman?"

"Yeah."

The two flirted back and forth, as Jay pumped his gas. The conversation began to veer in an intimate direction for the first time. When Jay got in the car and started it, the windshield wipers wouldn't budge. He played with the switch a few seconds but still got nothing.

"Fuck!" he vented.

"What's wrong?"

"Damn windshield wipers not coming on."

"Wow, you're not having the best day are you?"

"Not at all," Jay agreed.

He continued to turn the windshield wipers off and on, but it was an obvious waste of time.

"They still not coming on?"

"Nah, they won't budge. Damn."

"Well, you can't drive without wipers in that mess. Do you have a road side service number?"

"Yeah. Let me find it in my wallet and I'll call you back."

"Okay."

Michelle hung up the phone and realized her blouse was still halfway off and halfway on her shoulder because the phone had rang while she was undressing. She hadn't moved from that one spot since she had answered the phone. Instead of undressing, she slipped the blouse back on her shoulder in case Jay needed a ride or something. She sat on the side of her bed distracting herself with the television, waiting for him to call back. About ten minutes passed before she got irritated with her indecision on whether to take off her clothes or keep them on.

She decided to called Jay back, and he quickly answered.

"Hey. Did you get in touch with anybody?" she asked.

"Yeah. The dude I talked with said it sounds like the motor on the wipers is gone. They said if I can't drive it, they'll send a tow truck to come get it, but I won't be able to get another car until tomorrow."

"Did you need me to come pick you up?" she offered.

Jay had been sitting at the station trying to decide his next move when the phone rang. When Michelle offered to pick him up, it was a no brainer.

"You sure you wouldn't mind coming out in this mess?"

"Well, I don't wanna leave you stranded at the gas station," she said honestly.

Lines was the only person in the area he could call to come pick him up, and he'd be damn if he was going to be responsible for Lines any more tonight.

"Okay, well yeah, how soon can you get here?"

"Where are you?"

"Mack and Moross, near the hospital."

"Right, okay. Give me thirty or forty minutes."

"Okay."

~~~

Michelle arrived at the gas station at the same time as the tow truck. The rain was still coming down, and Jay was glad he had taken her up on her offer. They sat in her truck while the rental car was being hooked to the back of the tow truck, still flirting and enjoying each other, although it had been a crazy day for Jay. The tow truck driver jotted down all of Jay's insurance information and told him he was good to go.

"Don't be trying to come to my rescue, it's supposed to be the other way around." Jay said.

"I don't play that gender roles crap, I'm a superwoman," she shot back.

Jay laughed at her, but he was feeling her confidence. "What now?" Michelle asked, pulling out of the gas station into traffic with an unknown destination.

"I would say let's finish our date, but it's coming down too bad out here."

"Yeah, and I don't wanna keep driving around out here in this mess, you dig?" she teased.

"Aye, you can't be using my shit all willy nilly, like that."

Michelle burst into laughter as Jay sat with a straight face, as if he meant every word. She was glad to be in his presence again, and the night was still young.

"I won't use it again. I promise. Your lingo is not quite my style."

"Okay, we'll see. Anyway, I got an idea," Jay offered.

"I'm all ears."

"Either my place or yours," he chanced. But keep in mind, my house is in St. Clair Shores."

Michelle knew in the pouring rain it would take way too long to get to his house. Plus, the drive home would be even more draining. She thought it over as she cruised in the middle lane.

"Hmmm," she released. Jay sat in silence waiting on a response. "You know what? Fuck it," she heard herself say as she put on her blinker and veered in the turning lane headed back to her loft downtown.

CHAPTER 14

A huge sense of accomplishment came over Jay as soon as he crossed the threshold of the front door. He had played all his cards just right, and he'd be damned if it didn't land him right where he wanted to be. He took in the crème and white theme of the front room. The crème colored sofa with the lambskin throw complimented the white Persian rug under the glass-encased coffee table. There was a wine cabinet in the dining room filled with red wine. Jay strolled over to the wine cabinet as Michelle set down her clutch and keys then started to remove her heels.

"Now why do you have all this wine if you don't even drink?" he asked.

"It's called decor. Besides, I didn't say never ever."

Jay grabbed a bottle of Sutter Home sweet red wine.

"Well good. Let's make tonight a special occasion."

"What's the occasion?" she asked with a grin.

"The occasion is I made it inside your crib."

"Ha! You know what, you're right. That definitely is a special occasion. But come back over this way, because this front room is far as you're going to go," she assured.

While she went to the kitchen and grabbed some wine glasses and a corkscrew, Jay slid his pistol under the couch on the floor, just before Michelle came back to the spacious front room. She set the corkscrew down then gave Jay the glasses and turned on the flat screen.

~~~

Lines tried to go to sleep, but he was too riled up from all the coke he had done earlier that day. When Jay hit him with five bricks on consignment, Lines went straight Scarface with the package. He was done getting high for the night, but he found himself back in his truck on the way to the club for a couple of drinks. He knew he should probably call Ray Ray and the goons to roll out with him, but he ignored his gut instinct because he just didn't give a fuck about anything at the moment. The coke had him feeling invincible, and he thought if he could go have a couple drinks and maybe get some head, some pussy, or both, he could finally pass out and get some sleep. He ended up back at his same spot in the hood called Radoe's where the girls were always loose and ready.

"Bartender. Don Julio!" Lines shouted over the music with one finger raised in the air.

A pretty young thing slid beside him, almost invading his personal space while looking for the bartender. They locked eyes.

"Hello," the pretty lady spoke.

"Hey sexy, what you drinking?" Lines flirted.

~~~

Jay and Michelle settled on The Original Kings of Comedy as their movie pick for the night. They shared some gut busting laughs while sipping wine and enjoying each other's company. Jay sang along with Steve Harvey as he belted out old school songs Jay remembered hearing as a child in his household. He was being silly, but Michelle quickly realized he didn't sound half bad.

"Don't spill that wine on my sofa, R Kelly," she teased as he cupped the glass still singing.

As the night went on, Michelle was comfortable enough to have a second glass of wine, knowing full well she'd be tipsy afterwards. She had decided to not overthink the night and just let it flow.

Jay, on the other hand, had been staring down her blouse all night and was feeling frisky inside as he poured the last of the wine in his glass. He was physical-

ly and mentally attracted to Michelle, which was something he hadn't felt in years. He believed she felt the
same way, but wasn't one hundred percent certain, so he
asked.

"Be honest with me. Do you think we could have
something real?"

She took a sip of wine and set the glass down, letting
the question steep in her thoughts for a moment.

"I think if we are real with one another, we have no
choice but to establish something real," she replied.

"I agree."

"It's been a long time since a man has been inside my
home, so the fact that you made it here says a lot."

Jay paused for a moment, reading between the lines.

"I'm not perfect," he said, looking into her eyes.

"No one is asking you to be."

Jay thought if he let the moment pass, he may never
get a better opportunity than the one he had in front of
him. He could no longer contain his yearning desire, so
he leaned in and kissed her soft lips. They met him with
inviting pleasure. Their first kiss was wildly magical, and
it continued until Michelle realized he still had the cup in
his hand perched right over her Persian rug.

"Time out," she said, using a real referee signal with
her hands. "Because if you spill that wine, we are gonna
fight."

"Ha. We don't want that. Definitely can't have that," he replied setting the glass down slowly and moving in for another kiss.

Jay could tell the wine had taken its desired effect on Michelle. It went straight to her hormones and she was kissing him with so much passion, he reached in and pulled her closer. His lips and hands began to venture all over the places he had been dying to touch since their first date. He nibbled at the top of her breast while his hand slid down and cupped her Jell-O soft ass. As he continued to explore her amazing body, Jay developed a hard on that couldn't wait to breathe. Michelle's hands rubbed up and down his slender, but rock solid physique as the twinkle between her thighs began to ignite with every touch. The way he roamed her body felt like he was born to do it; like it was his purpose in life.

Before she knew it, her blouse was completely open and he had managed to get her nipples out of her bra and into his mouth. She leaned back into the arm of the couch, massaging his head with one hand as she rubbed his rock hard erection with the other. At that moment, she knew this thing was going all the way, and she wanted it. She wanted it bad.

When they finally unlocked, Michelle stood up and removed her blouse while Jay pulled his shirt over his head and dropped it to the floor. Michelle stood there with the most beautiful set of C cups he'd ever laid eyes on.

"Come on," she beckoned toward the bedroom. "You got a condom, right?"

"Hell yeah," Jay said excitedly.

"Okay, come on," she said and crooked her finger again.

Jay quick-stepped, watching her ass make Jell-O like motions as he moved in the direction of the bedroom. He caught up to her, grabbing her by the waist in the hallway, and slid his tongue down her throat. She kissed him back long and hard, while Jay slid his hand up her dress and pulled her panties down. He palmed her ass cheeks as she released his belt buckle and undid his jeans. Realizing they may or may not make it to the bedroom, Jay grabbed the condom and quickly placed it on. He lifted her leg as she held onto his shoulders and the wall for balance, and he slowly eased inside her.

He kissed her collarbone while she moaned in pleasure. The hypnotic rhythm of their bodies collided with pure ecstasy. He went deeper inside of her goodness with every stroke. She could feel her G spot being tampered with and she gripped him tighter. Her fingernails dug into his back, and she screamed obscenities as her body began to stiffen, sending them both into orgasmic convulsions. It was good to the very last drop. When it was over, the two stood panting heavily in the hallway with Jay still holding her left leg in the air.

"See," Michelle said out of breath. "I told you, you wouldn't make it past the front room."

~~~

An hour after he left the club, Lines had the pretty young thing he'd met earlier face down and ass up, giving her back shots at a rinky dink hotel on the east side. She screamed rehearsed dirty talk like a professional porn queen, giving Lines all the motivation he needed to pound her out until he climaxed with a body-quivering nut. As soon as he busted off, Lines pulled the condom off and went to the bathroom to pee. When he turned his back, Oshiwa looked at the time on the hotel clock. It was 1:59am, and she should have been dressed and ready by now.

"Fuck!" she fumed, rolling out of the bed completely naked. She ran to the door and quickly unlocked it.

Lines heard the deadbolts unlocking, and he immediately knew he had finally fucked up one too many times making bad decisions. When he stepped into the hallway to see what the girl was doing, Los was already inside with his gun out. Still completely naked, Lines tried to break for the gun under his pillow, but Los had the drop. There was nothing he could do but brace for the impact as the bullets from the 40-caliber pistol ripped through his flesh and spun him around before he fell to his knees and the bed broke his fall. His torso stretched out across the bed as he laid face down.

Los put another hot one in the back of his head. He tossed the bag of bones, and turned to look at Oshiwa, who was scurrying to find her clothes.

"Why the fuck you ain't dressed?" he yelled.

"Cause the nigga was taking forever to buss a nut, shit!" she shouted back. "Hold on."

Oshiwa wiggled into her pants as quickly as possible, afraid of being caught at the scene of a homicide.

"Hold on my ass, I'm outta here," Los said walking out of the front door.

He didn't make it five steps before he found himself at gunpoint, staring at killers with no mercy. Gunner and Ray Ray squeezed off round after round, sending Carlos crashing into and over the third story guardrail. The sound of his bones cracking and his body banging against the pavement was enough to make Gunner cringe a little inside. He peeked over the rail to view the body then he and Ray Ray went inside the room to search for the girl, but all they found was Lines' dead body bleeding all over the mattress.

Ray Ray stormed in the bathroom and found the window open that led to a balcony on the other side. He rushed back out of the bathroom.

"Come on, that bitch climbed out the window."

They ran out the room and to the car as fast as possible, bailing out of the parking lot at top speed. Gunner was behind the wheel, and he flew up and down the nearby blocks trying to catch up with the conniving bitch that had just got Lines killed. They didn't even know what she looked like, but they knew she'd be running scared and probably drawing a lot of attention to herself.

"Bitch!" Gunner banged on the steering wheel as he drove frantically up and down the blocks. "Why the fuck didn't I follow my first mind?"

Gunner had talked to Lines right before he left the club, and he knew exactly where he was headed. Since he couldn't stop Lines from doing what he wanted to do, he wanted to check on him after hearing about him spazzing out at Niecey Girl's house. Since he and Ray Ray were already together at a dice game, they decided to check on Lines. But deep down inside, Gunner felt that if he would have left the dice game when his intuition told him to, Lines would still be alive.

~~~

Bones got the call around 2:20am that Oshiwa was hiding in some bushes about ten blocks away from the hotel. All she had was her jeans and her cell phone. When the shooting started right outside the door, she was forced to flee the scene, leaving everything including the rest of her clothes. She called Bones again about ten minutes later, after finding out the name of the street she was on. When Bones was finally riding up the block, he called her and she quickly answered.

"I'm coming up the block now," Bones said.

"Where? I don't see you," she said squinting as she looked up the block.

"You see me now? Flicking the light?"

"Okay, yeah I see you. Come down to the middle of the next block."

Oshiwa had been laid out behind the front bushes of a stranger's yard for almost an hour, being drenched with rain and bitten by mosquitos. She ran to the car as fast as she could, holding her bare breasts in her forearms. As soon as she was in the car, Bones sped off. He knew if Los was already dead, somebody was probably looking for her. Bones looked at Oshiwa and could tell she was more shaken up by the experience than even she had expected.

"You aiight?" he asked.

"Hell no, I ain't aiight! That shit wasn't supposed to go like that. I almost died!"

"How the fuck they knew y'all was there?"

"I don't fucking know. All I know is soon as Carlos went outside the door, some niggas was waiting and they shot his ass."

Bones hated to lose a shooter like Carlos, but truthfully, he was expendable. Sometimes it's a life for a life in the game of war.

CHAPTER 15

Michelle was called in earlier than expected the next morning. She dropped Jay off at the rental car company just as the doors opened for business. It was amazing having a man in her bed with his arms wrapping her up all night long. The only bad thing was Jay seemed a little detached on the ride over. They shared a small kiss and he got out without even a goodbye. What she didn't know was that Jay had ten missed calls on his phone, and he knew something was seriously wrong. He also knew it was something he couldn't discuss in front of her, so he was waiting until she was gone to return the calls. He called Gunner back while still standing on the outside of the building.

Gunner picked up fast. "Dog!"

"What up?" Jay said, bracing himself. The tone of Gunner's voice said it all before he even spoke another word.

"They got Lines, man!"

"Got Lines? Lines went home last night."

"Naw man, somebody hit 'em."

"Lines dead?" he asked for confirmation as the tension quickly started to build inside of him.

"Yeah Jay... he dead."

"Fuck!" He shouted, hanging up the phone. He walked through the parking lot squeezing the phone in his hand so hard his palm turned blood red.

"Fuck, fuck, fuck!"

He continued to wander around the parking lot confused until he realized he didn't have a car to get in and pull off. He turned around and headed back toward the building. He looked dangerous to the other customers walking by as his mind was being mauled by fast and individual images of what could have happened to Lines. He started to call Gunner back but stopped himself. He had to gain some kind of composure. He had to go inside and get the rental car first, and then he could go straight to Gunner and talk to him face to face. He inhaled deeply, wiping his hands over his face. He gathered himself the best he could and headed inside to speak with a service rep.

~~~

Michelle had two hours to prepare for a news story about a double homicide that took place at a hotel on the eastside the night before. When she was done with that, she had to immediately begin working on another story that had to been completed before the four o'clock news. It was a hectic life sometimes being a reporter, but she was always up for the challenge.

Her crew arrived at the scene of the crime just an hour before they were supposed to go live. That didn't give her much time to do her pre-interviews, but she did the best she could. She talked to the hotel manager who was working at the time of the incident, as well as the homicide detective working the case. After a few more phone calls, she felt she had a strong grasp of what had happened and what she was allowed to report and what to leave out.

After some last minute hair and make-up touch ups inside the news van, she moved briskly to her shooting area, knowing she was only moments away from going live. Once in position, she had about a minute and half of down time. She hated the down time when she just had to stand there waiting to go live.

"This is Michelle Mitchell, reporting live from the scene of a grizzly double homicide at the Bridgemount Hotel right on east Jefferson. Right now, police say the details are sketchy, but it appears that the shooting might have been a planned ambush. Witnesses say they heard a series of shots fired from inside the hotel room, and then another barrage of bullets outside the hotel seconds later. When it was all over, one man was found dead in his hotel room and another man, who police believe fell from the third floor was found dead on the first floor."

~~~

Bones and Skip had Oshiwa's home looking more like a trap house than anything these days. Digital scales could be found scattered all through the house, along with boxes of sandwich bags, Ziploc storage bags and random rubber bands. Skip stood in the kitchen over the stove cooking crack, while Bones and Oshiwa smoked a blunt as he teased her about last night's events.

"It don't matter. I did it though. I got it done," she said, defending her right to be shaken up after everything that had taken place. No one really spoke of Carlos and his death, with the exception of the news reports. It was like he never existed to them. Since Carlos was only a hired gun, no one felt the loss, and life went on as usual.

"Did you give 'em some head though?" Bones asked with a grin, referring to Lines.

"I mean, I did what I had to do. You sent me on a mission, I did what I had to do," she explained.

"I'm just asking did you give him some head."

"You know she gave him said head, nigga. Quit talking stupid," Skip shouted from the kitchen after eavesdropping on the conversation.

"Yeah, I gave that nigga some head. He asked me to. I wouldn't have just did it if he didn't ask, but he asked," she said with a shrug.

For some reason, Bones felt something about her sucking Lines' dick, but nothing about her fucking him. He wouldn't make a fuss about it, but he felt a bit disrespected.

"What time you going shopping?" he said, changing the subject.

"Whatever time you give me some money."

"What? You got money, whatchu talking 'bout?"

"I know I do, but I wanna spend your money, nigga. I just went to hell and back for your ass. I shouldn't even have to ask."

What could Bones say? He knew he needed Oshiwa more than anyone on his squad. He passed her the blunt, went in his pocket, and pulled out a bankroll of five thousand dollars. He gave her two thousand and she cupped her hand back and forth, signaling for more. He peeled off another five hundred shaking his head.

"Now it's something else I been meaning to talk to y'all about," she started.

"What's that?"

"How much y'all be paying for the work?" she inquired.

"Who sent you?" Skip shouted from the kitchen.

"Nigga shut up. I'm serious."

"I'm serious too. Who sent you?" he teased, making Bones chuckle.

"Aiight, y'all joking, but I'm so serious right now. I think I could probably get it cheaper," she announced.

"Yeah right," Bones said waving her off.

"Okay. I see you still underestimating me. Why?"

Bones could see she was dead serious now, and she had his attention. It just didn't seem like she would have something like this under her hat all this time and not mention it.

"So, how about this? How about you tell me how much you can get 'em for?" he said, not wanting to reveal the price he was already paying to her.

"I'm not sure. It's been a minute, I'd have to call and find out."

"Is you fucking with me, girl?" Bones said.

Skip was done in the kitchen, so he came out and joined them in the living room.

"Where you get a plug from all of sudden?" Skip asked.

"It's not all of sudden, he been around. I just wanted to make sure I was gonna be treated right before I spoke on it."

"Okay, so who is the plug?" Bones asked, now dying to know who this mystery man was.

"Dontae's old plug. The mayor's son.

Skip's eyes grew wide, and Bones just looked confused. Bones had been away, and he didn't know much about the mayor or his son. Dawson was an eastside dude, and most of the hustlers he supplied were also, but Skip knew of him. Skip also knew that if Oshiwa was being truthful, her connect was worth investigating.

"She talking about this cat named Dawson. I heard about him," Skip confirmed.

"Oh yeah? So where you know him from?" Bones asked.

"From Dontae. You keep acting like I'm new to this or something," she said with attitude.

"You got a number for this nigga?" Bones asked.

Oshiwa got up and stomped out of the room with even more attitude. She was upset that she wasn't being taken seriously. A minute later, she came back with a little black book and flopped down next to Bones. She thumbed through the pages until she found what she was looking for.

Stabbing at the number with her index finger, she said, "Right here. Dawson."

CHAPTER 16

All Jay could think about was Lines and J-Rock as he drove to the hood to meet with Gunner and the rest of his crew. He wondered who the triggerman was. It had been a good seven years since he'd seen Bones face to face, but he still held a vivid picture of the enemy's face locked in his mind. This wasn't the first time he'd lost a friend to the game or street war, but never had he felt so directly responsible for it. He had known Lines all his life, and had practically raised J-Rock. He felt a rising lump in his throat when he thought of Lines laid out dead on a hotel floor. He felt something inside he had never felt before. Jay felt... defeated. This was the part of the game he had discussed with his pops on many occasions, and he wished he could pick up the phone and call him at that very moment.

When Jay pulled up to the house Gunner used to hide women from his wife, he saw so many cars outside he knew everyone was already there.

He didn't know what anyone was driving these days, but that's the way it had to be. When he walked in, the lump in throat returned as he stared into the eyes, of Bake, E, Gunner and Ray Ray.

"I told that nigga to stay out of the fucking street," Jay scolded in frustration.

"I hate to say it man, but Lines got his own self killed. He left the club with a set up bitch. He didn't know that bitch from a can of paint," Gunner informed.

"What the nigga look like that shot him?"

"Light skin nigga, that's all I remember. I never seen him before."

Jay's cell phone rang and he saw it was Dawson. He was probably calling about some new shit he just got in, about to brag on his product as usual. Jay didn't have time for his nonsense, so his ignored the call.

"I can't believe we just letting niggas pick us off like this, dog," Jay continued. "Ray Ray, you ain't found nothing about this nigga Bones yet?"

"Naw man, but I'ma tell you like this. Y'all say the nigga got family all around this bitch. If we can't find him, I say we find the next best thing. You know I don't give a fuck, Jay, I'll kill kids and all if need be."

"Naw, we ain't killing no kids, Ray Ray, that ain't gonna bring Lines back."

Ray Ray was a cold blooded killer, and he was ready to put in work to show just how valuable he was to the team.

"I hear you, Jay, but nothing we gone do is gone bring Lines back. Meantime, we need to show muthafuckas we the last niggas in the world they wanna beef with. If you don't wanna get the kids, that's cool. I'll get sisters, mamas, uncles, cousins." Ray Ray was hype now. "You know me, I'm a dog. Put my food in a bowl and slide that shit in the corner on the floor, 'cause I'm a muthafucking dog! And I ain't with watching my niggas die."

Ray Ray was bringing a much needed energy into the room. Just when Jay was beginning to feel like he had no one, he realized he had some of the coldest killers in the D on his squad. Ray Ray came with a small crew of his own, all gutter just like him. It was definitely time to let them earn their stripes. First, they had to sniff out the enemy's trail.

~~~

The next few days were bittersweet for Michelle. On one hand, she was extremely excited about the opportunities that lay ahead. She had gotten the word that she and Andrea would be filling in for Diane on the evening news as possible candidates to fill her position when she left the station. Apparently, all Andrea's brownnosing was paying off after all. On the other hand, she hadn't heard from Jay since the morning she dropped him off at the rental car company. Inside, she felt unbelievably stupid, and it was taking her off her A game. She sat at a Starbucks on her lunch break contemplating what could have possibly gone wrong, and how she should handle it from here. She called Leslie to confess and to hopefully get some guidance.

"Hey, love of my life," Leslie answered.

"If I'm the love of your life, whose ring are you wearing?"

"Oh hush. Be glad somebody loves you."

"You don't know the half," Michelle said, feeling underappreciated.

"Why, what's wrong?

"Huuuuuuh," she sighed. "Where do I start?"

"How about the beginning?" Leslie said with concern in her tone.

"Okay, so me and Jay hit it off really, really well, as you know."

"Right?"

"Everything was going perfectly until I made the mistake of getting caught up in a moment and moving too fast. To make a long story short... I slept with him"

"Wow."

"Yes, and that was three days ago and I haven't heard from him since then."

"No!"

"Yes! And it's driving me crazy because you know I would never in a million years just sleep with someone I didn't really think I saw a serious possibility of being with. So right now I'm going through quite an array of emotions."

"You should call him," Leslie suggested.

"What? No."

"Yes. Call him, because you could be getting yourself worked all up over nothing. Things happen, you know? Maybe he lost his phone or maybe something is going on with him you don't know about. Just call him."

Michelle thought about the last time they were together and how they flew out of the Fox theatre in the middle of the play.

"Maybe you're right, but I just don't wanna call him and find out that he really has just been avoiding me, then I'll really feel like shit."

"I don't believe that's it. I mean, what man in his right mind would settle for one night with you when you were clearly offering more?"

"Well thanks, I really needed to hear that. I still don't know about calling him though," she admitted.

"That's because you're all in your feelings right now. Just call the man, and when you find out you were wrong, you can call me back and tell me I was right."

Michelle pondered her next move.

"If you're wrong I'm never taking your advice again."

"Oh, but I'm so right. Call the man. And congrats on making lead anchor, I'm claiming it early."

"Thanks. Love you."

"Love you more. Bye.

"Bye.

Michelle hung up, still petrified of making the call. Rejection from men was something she had no experience with, and the thought of it was terrifying. She clutched her cellphone, tapping her nails on the table. *Get out of your feelings; she's right, you're a hell of a catch. Just call him.*

Michelle decided it would be worse to continue the day waiting and wondering, so she decided to call. She dialed Jay's number and it rang. It rang again. It continued to ring, until finally, the voicemail picked up. She didn't have a thought out message to leave, because she had called on the spur of the moment, so she hung up. She sat in Starbucks waiting for a call back the rest of her lunch break, but it never came. How badly she wanted to drive to Leslie and choke her right now.

~~~

Jay was in the middle of passing out the new bulletproof vests he had just bought for everybody when he looked at his cellphone and saw that Michelle had called him. It was such bad timing that he'd met someone he actually could see a future with, and now he didn't even want to have a simple phone conversation with her. There was nothing else on his mind but the current situation that needed to be dealt with. He knew Michelle was probably worried that she had done something wrong, or probably just extremely confused. He promised himself he wouldn't avoid her for much longer. She didn't deserve that, but right now his mind was running rampant.

They had been in Bones' old neighborhood all week trying to come up with something or somebody to leak some information or blood, one or the other. But they had come up empty handed. Meantime, business still had to be handled, but as the day of Lines' funeral approached, Jay's mind was clouded and somewhat disoriented as he went about his day. Dawson had continued to call him, and had even left a voicemail on his answering machine, sounding upset about not receiving a call back. As far as Jay was concerned, their business was done, so fuck Dawson and his feelings. He had bigger fish to fry. Truth be told, it was dangerous to still try to hustle with so much serious beef on the floor, but Jay knew if he let Bones stop their hustle, he will truly have won the war.

That night, the crew met up again at Niecey Girl's house to turn in money to Jay and to put together some funds for Lines' family that would be passed out after the funeral. Jay still felt like his nuts were in a vise, and he was just sitting around waiting for someone else from his crew to get whacked. Not being a drinker, he felt lost when he found himself turning to alcohol to comfort his state of confusion. He had a bottle of Don Julio, and he was using a toast to Lines as his excuse, knowing it was his favorite drink. The truth was, he just needed to calm himself by any means necessary.

"I gotta get this feeling off of me, dog. I don't care how many people gotta die," he admitted, throwing a shot back.

"I know it feel like we lying down right now, nigga, but we gone take it to that bitch ass nigga sooner than later. This city ain't that big, trust me," Gunner assured him.

"I can't think straight." Jay said, pouring another shot and passing the bottle around. "Everybody get a shot, man, so we can toast to the memory of my muthafucking dog, ya dig? Both my niggas, matter of fact. We gon set this city on fire about my niggas. Teach these bitch ass niggas who to play with, ya dig?"

Jay continued to talk himself into believing he could win a war with a ghost. If there was a will, there was a way, and he would find it. After drinking the first bottle, Bake left and came back with another bottle, and the crew sat around drinking and reminiscing until well after midnight. Jay being the only lightweight in the room, was certifiably drunk. As they all prepared to leave at the same time, Jay even staggered a little.

"You might wanna stay here tonight, 'cause you look drunk," Niecey Girl said.

"Naw, I spent the night here last night. I'm going home," he slurred.

"Okay. You grown," Niecey Girl said, leaving it alone.

As everyone piled outside, Jay staggered again, and this time Bake saw it too.

"Man, you sure you can drive, dog?"

"When have I ever been unable to drive, Bake?" Jay said, getting upset.

"Never. But when have I ever asked until now?"

"I'm straight, dog. I'm straight. I'm about to take my ass home and get in the bed."

"Aiight man, call me and let me know you made it or something."

"Yup."

Jay climbed behind the wheel of his rental Camaro and started it up. He backed out of the driveway and went flying up the residential street like he was drag racing.

Bake was worried.

On the freeway, Jay drove like a lunatic, dipping in and out of lanes, doing over a hundred miles an hour. He petrified motorists to the point that everyone just moved out of his way to let him pass. His music was blasting and Young Jeezy's song, "Gangsta Music" had a hypnotizing effect on his mood as he plotted military minded war strategies. He gunned past a state trooper parked in the shoulder with no lights on. It was too late to slow down, but after spotting the trooper's car, he did it anyway.

Jay could see the trooper in his rearview mirror with his red and blue flashing lights, but he didn't slow down any more than he already had. He contemplated running. He was drunk, wearing a bulletproof vest, and carrying a pistol. If he stopped, he was going to jail, no doubt about it. He stomped the gas and switched over to the last lane so he could exit the freeway.

At the first available exit ramp, he rolled down his window and slung the pistol as he bent the corner at the same time.

The state trooper got off on the same exit and was still behind him. Jay bent another hard right, barely missing the tail end of a black Bronco. He swerved around the Bronco and into the far right turning lane. The state trooper was about four cars back, and Jay knew that more were probably on the way. He turned left, down a residential street, and the back end of his Camaro spun out and fishtailed before he got control and stabbed off again. He could hear the number of sirens doubling. Tripled now. Getting closer. He spotted a patrol car setting up to block his path at the end of the next block.

He slowed down, trying to think quickly, but now the state trooper was really on his ass, close enough to ram him if he wanted. Jay thought of surrendering, but decided against it. He yanked the wheel and jumped the curb, but the wheels spun out, hitting freshly watered grass, and he had trouble getting traction.

More police cars lined the block.

Jay had no way out as he drove up the sidewalk until he had no choice but to slam on brakes, or ram a squad car head on. He slammed on his brakes as police jumped out and approached the car with weapons drawn. Jay put his hands in the air in surrender, and police snatched the door open and dragged him from the car.

"Don't fucking move! Matter of fact, move so I can blow your fucking head off!" A Detroit police officer yelled.

Jay knew it wasn't just a threat, so he remained stiff as a board and they cuffed him quickly and snatched him from the ground. As they shoved him in the backseat of the State trooper's car, a calm came over Jay as they began to search his vehicle. He knew there was nothing in the car, and whatever charges he was facing, he'd surely be out in a day or two. Still, he had to face the fact that his life was spiraling out of control.

CHAPTER 17

Sitting in the slammer at some precinct on the westside of town that he'd never seen before, Jay tried unsuccessfully to get some rest on the cold hard cement. He wasn't able to reach his lawyer with his one phone call, so he called Niecey Girl and told her what happened and what to do. He looked around at some the other degenerates of society and felt trapped. He wasn't charged for the bulletproof vest, but he was charged with alluding and reckless endangerment. He knew the vest was illegal, but it wasn't something they pushed to prosecute normally, unless it was attached to crime involving a firearm.

Jay wasn't upset about the charges because he'd brought it on himself. He was more upset that he had put himself in the position he was in. The dude in the cell to the left of him looked like he had to be a dope fiend. The dude to the right of him was a loud mouth with a domestic violence charge, who kept proclaiming his innocence the entire time he was there. The story made no logical sense whatsoever.

"I was just wiping her face with a towel, man. Then police walk in talking about get your hand off her. Talking 'bout you choking her. I said 'I'm wiping her face,' what is you talking about?"

The youngster in the cell directly across from Jay listened attentively since he had nothing better to do. After hearing the whole story, the youngster put his two cents in.

"Yeah man, I think you need to get her on the phone and have her come down here and talk to your arresting officer."

"She won't accept none of my calls," the man explained.

That's probably because you choked the shit out of her, Jay thought.

"Just keep trying to contact her, dog. You'll be straight," the youngster said. "I know I'ma be good soon as I get a bond. I don't care what it is, my nigga, Bones, gone come get me. My nigga getting that bread, but he need me. I'm the best worker he got. He just copped that Lexus 460 though. Getting long money. He low-key with his shit though. He come through and pick up that bread, and be out."

Jay listened quietly as the young thug boasted about his boss, who it appeared was the man Jay had searched up and down for over the past few days. He calculated a plan right then. Choosing his words carefully, he hopped up off the concrete slab and strolled to the bars.

"Aye, young dog. You say your man name Bones?"

"Yeah."

"Sound like my man I was locked up with. Who he run with?" Jay asked.

"Shiiid, he mainly be with Skip, or the little bad bitch. Her name Oshiwe or some shit like that."

"Yeah... I know Skip too. Them my mans from PA."

"Hell yeah, that's all us, nigga. PA for life, we bout to be running shit over there."

"They call me Snoop. What you go by on the streets?" Jay asked.

"They call me Pistol Pete, 'cause I keep that thang on me, you feel me?"

"Yeah, I feel that. I ain't seen my man since he went to Ohio and caught that bid," Jay continued to bait the young thug.

"Yeah, that nigga been out for a minute now. 'Bout four or five months. Came straight home taking care of his business, you know? Bounced back quick like what? Shining on the bums."

Jay had heard enough of his dick riding, so he change the subject.

"So where y'all set up at?" he asked, reeling him in.

"We all around that muthafucka. We got a spot on Mansfield down the street from Skip house. We got a spot on Sunsex—"

"Skip live on Mansfield?" Jay interrupted.

"Yeah, he on the first block off Puritan. Skip just dropped the Audi. Cold. Threw twenty-twos on that bitch."

This nigga is super stupid, Jay thought. The more he talked, it was like taking candy from a baby. He wondered if the dude knew where Bones lived, but he didn't want to go overboard with the questions and make him suspicious. It was best to just let him keep running his mouth.

"So what you in for, young dog?" he said, switching subjects again.

I got swooped on walking down hot ass Linwood with a burner on me, that's all. This my third one, so I know my bond gone be high as hell, but Bones coming to get a nigga, so I ain't worried."

"Yeah. I should be outta here in the morning myself."

After a few more words, Jay went back to his cement block and began to strategize his next move. He thought back to the conversation he'd had with Gunner just yesterday. Gunner was right, the city wasn't that big. Not that big at all.

~~~

The next morning, Jay and Pistol Pete were shackled and cuffed together, and they were transferred from the holding cell with six others to the police van that would escort them to the courthouse. The dude in for domestic violence was really in a panic now that they were about to go before a judge. He was gathering as much information about the working of the court system and his chances of going to prison or doing county time. After listening to him all night long, Jay was at the end of his rope with this guy, and he refused to listen any longer.

"Man, why don't you shut the fuck up and just wait and see."

The look on Jay's face was enough to know he meant business and was about to snap. That put an end to all questions from him for the rest of the ride over. At the courthouse, Pistol Pete was the first called in front of a judge. He got hit with a seventy-five thousand ten percent bond, which meant he seventy-five hundred cash to post bail. He came back to the holding cell unruffled.

"I'll be out in a minute," he said with confidence.

Jay went in front the judge next. His lawyer had gotten the message, and was there to represent him with the same beat up looking hard bottoms he always wore.

"I see you got the message," Jay said.

"Yeah. Shit, Keith woke me up at five-thirty in the morning to make sure I got it."

Gunner, Niecey Girl and E sat in the back of the courtroom waiting patiently. The judge was an older red head white woman with a permanent scowl, but she was actually a pretty fair judge. The arraignment was swift, and Dan Marsh spoke on Jay's behalf, getting his bond set at twenty thousand. The bond was immediately paid and Jay was out in the next hour.

Once out of jail, Jay quickly set his plan in motion, knowing it was risky and only had a fifty percent chance of working. He hugged Niecey Girl and sent her home quickly. Then, he went back in the courthouse with E and Gunner. They stood in a line of people whispering amongst each other, going over all the details. Gunner had several fake IDs so he was the one elected to post Pistol Pete's Bond. They paid the seventy-five hundred, but by the time it posted, Pete had already been sent over to the county jail. They waited patiently for the county processing to take place, and then Pete would emerge out of the front door. The worst thing that could happen is that Bones and Skip actually showed up to get him before they could nab him, but that would be even better.

Two hours passed before Pete came strolling out of the county jail revolving door with a winning smile on his face. He searched around for whoever was bonding him out, and he looked confused as he headed toward the parking lot and didn't see any cars that resembled Bones' or Skip's vehicles. Jay got out of the passenger seat of Gunner's rental car and waved him over.

Pete looked shocked, but not suspicious. He jogged across the street to the parking lot with a grin on his face. They slapped fives. Gunner and E were friendly.

"You bonded me?"

"Yeah. I told you them my niggas too. Where you need to go, man? We can drop you off?"

"I gotta get back to the hood. PA, you already know."

"Let's go," Jay said and they all hopped in.

"Man, I can't thank you enough, Snoop. That was love, dog." Pete said gratefully.

"Ain't nothing man, I'm glad I could help."

"You got that coming right back too, soon as I get in touch with Bones."

"Yeah, I know you good for it."

"Matter fact, let me borrow somebody cellphone. Mine is dead as a doorknob."

The car was deadly silent. No music, no responses. Nothing.

"They impounded my car with my cellphone in it," Jay said truthfully."

"What about you, homeboy?" Pete asked E sitting in the backseat next to him.

"Man, I just lost my cellphone yesterday. I gotta go buy me one," E lied.

"Shit, I just tried to make a call. My battery dead as fuck," Gunner said before he could even ask.

Jay could sense Pete's uneasiness began to set in as he glanced at him in the rearview mirror."

"We can stop at a pay phone somewhere. Let's just get the fuck away from downtown," Jay said.

"Yeah, that's cool. I just wanna let niggas know I'm out so they don't waste a trip down here, you feel me? Plus, I know you want that bread back."

"Yeah, we can make an extra stop somewhere. We gotta make one stop anyway."

Gunner finally turned the music up, knowing everything was in motion. As he hit the freeway, Pete began to nod to the music, feeling relaxed. They came off the freeway after passing a few exits.

"There's a phone booth right there," Pete yelled over the music.

Jay turned the volume down.

"You can make some calls at the house we going to. We gotta make a little stop."

They turned down the block where Gunner's chill spot was. It was the only spot they had that no outsiders knew of. It was perfect for what they had planned. When Gunner pulled into the driveway, Jay immediately hoped out calm and cool.

"Come on, Pete."

Pete got out, but he was a little hesitant.

Gunner and E lay back for minute, just to make sure Pete went all the way inside. They didn't want to cause a scene outside where the neighbors could see. Murder wasn't exactly E's strong point, but in situations like this, it was kill or be killed. Once he was inside, they hopped out, looking around on the block as they rushed the side door, pulling pistols out.

Jay and Pete were in the middle of a conversation when E and Gunner stormed in.

"Where the pho—"

The three of them began to mob Pete. Jay punched him with his fist, and Gunner and E pistol-whipped him in the head. He fell to the floor and they continued to kick and stomp him until he was nearly unconscious. Even then, Jay continued to rear back and kick him in the ribs and stomach as hard as he could. His face was a bloody mess and he finally passed out in the middle of the kitchen floor. They dragged him legs first down the basement steps.

Jay checked his pulse and could tell he was still very much alive. Just unconscious. The look on E's face showed his amateur experience with this sort of thing. He just wanted to get it over with quickly as possible.

"Damn, we need his ass awake," Gunner said.

"Get some cold water," Jay told him. "E, go check outside and see what the neighbors doing. A few minutes later, Gunner came back down the steps carrying a bucket of cold water. What happened next was the most vile and ungodly act of vengeance Jay himself had ever committed. Before waking him, Pete was stripped of all of his clothing, and then doused with the cold water all over his body. He shook himself conscious from the shock of the cold water hitting his wounded face and body. His eyes were swollen shut and he had knots and gashes all over his head. Barely conscious, Pete tried to speak.

"What I... do ... Snoop?"

He knew he was about to die, and he just wanted to know why. Bones and Skip obviously were not letting their people know a whole lot about what was going on, but it worked to Jay's advantage.

"If you don't know by now, you shit out of luck. Now where's the house you roll at?"

"Mansfield."

"What block?" Jay barked. Pete was having trouble speaking, so Jay kicked him in his already broken ribs. "What block, muthafucka?"

"Ss- second block."

Pete answered every question he could to the best of his ability just to stop the assault. It was torture to be in that much pain and fear, and he would much rather just die.

"Where Bones live?"

"I... I don't... I don't know."

Jay held on to a beam for leverage and began to work his ribs with kick after kick.

"Where the fuck Bones live?"

Pete began to cough up blood, unable to answer because he couldn't speak, and simply didn't know the answer to Jay's question. Jay stormed upstairs frustrated and came back with E and a mop handle without the mop.

"Hold him still," he ordered Gunner and E.

They grabbed Pete and turned him on his stomach. As soon as the handle touched his anus, Pete mustered the strength to beg for mercy, but it was too late as Jay rammed up in him hard. The screams were loud enough to shatter the windows, and Gunner knew that it couldn't continue.

"That shit too loud, Jay," Gunner pleaded, releasing Pete's arm. The look in Jay's eyes was one of temporary insanity.

"If he knew more, he would have told us by now, Jay," E agreed, not wanting the sodomy to continue.

For a moment, Jay just stood there holding the mop handle, staring down at Pete as he whimpered like a wounded dog.

"Finish that bitch," Jay growled.

CHAPTER 18

Michelle was doing her best to have a good day, despite being frustrated with her personal life. Today was an important day, and she needed to be focused. It started on a positive note with her being handed all positive stories that warmed her heart as she worked. No murders, no violence, just positivity. Although her story on the new college grants for inner city youth was preceded by a man found dead rolled inside a rug on Mansfield Street, still it felt better when she wasn't the one blessed with the task of shedding light on all the violence taking place in the city. This was why the job she was up for meant so much to her. The change in position would mean she had more control, if only a morsel. More importantly, it would put her in a better position to do what she really wanted to do.

Michelle wanted the opportunity to explore the positive things about Detroit, and also explore what was being done about the not so positive things. Who was really to blame? Who was being held accountable? It could be done, but first she had to get more power and responsibility behind her title.

Today, she and Andrea had to do some test reels on the set from behind the desk, reading old stories from the teleprompter. After that, the tapes were to be turned in personally by them to the President of the Network News. To Michelle, it seemed a little unorthodox that the president was involving himself in the decision that was usually made by someone at the local level, but she went with it. The station was making no effort to hide the fact that she and Andrea were going head up for the position, which seemed a little unreal to Michelle. The last thing she could afford to do right now was dwell on Jay, but there he was like a monkey on her back, poking away at her thoughts.

Michelle watched from the floor as Andrea did her tape. She stumbled on a couple of simple words as if it was her first time in front of a camera. Michelle thought she seemed a little nervous, but an audition tape should have been a piece of cake—a mere formality. Then again, she didn't want to get too cocky and find herself screwing up.

"Just focus," she mumbled to herself, trying to push Jay to the back of her mind.

Andrea rose from behind the desk when she was done and went to talk with the cameraman. Michelle waited to be called, and then took her seat to begin her test on a health news story. She was very sharp and articulate, plus her personality really shined through. She nailed it, just like she believed she would.

After the test reels were done, there was some down time before the interview with the big man, so Andrea offered to buy Michelle lunch. *This should be interesting,* Michelle thought. It was right on the tip of her tongue to decline her invitation, but she ended up at the small downtown eatery near the station sitting across from Andrea and wondering why.

"So are you excited about the possibility of being lead anchor?" Andrea asked.

"Oh, of course. It's what I came here for, aren't you?"

"Well… for me it's just another step up the ladder. I mean, I want the job, but how far can you really go in Detroit, ya know?"

"I think you can go as far as you want to go," Michelle replied.

"I guess. I just think some people set their goals higher than others, that's all."

Michelle didn't respond to the comment, but she was mentally kicking herself for agreeing to do lunch with this arrogant, talentless heffa.

"Well, I wish you the highest of heights in all your endeavors, Andrea."

"Why thanks, and I wish you the same. You're such a sweetheart," she said with painted smile.

"Thanks, I try to be."

"You know, I'm curious as to why they're moving so fast with the interview process, when Diane's not supposed to be leaving for a few months."

"Well, if we're the only two people from the station they are considering, I'm guessing they want to get it out of the way in case neither one of us is a good fit, they can begin the search."

"I can't see them not picking either one of us," Andrea admitted.

"You never know," Michelle said with a shrug.

"I found in life, the people that climb the ladder the quickest are the ones that are willing to go the extra mile. Do whatever it takes.

Talking to Andrea sometimes was like doing a crossword puzzle the way Michelle had to examine each word.

"This ladder of success you speak of, where does it end?" she asked curiously.

"It doesn't end. But, I'll tell you where it starts. It starts with that lead anchor position."

"Listen, Andrea, just because we're going up for the same job it doesn't mean we have to become two women in constant competition with each other. There's plenty of room in the world for successful black women who are willing to work hard to get there."

"See, that's where you're wrong. Society is set up for men to rise to the top of their professions, while the women stand behind them. America is set up for the white man to rise to the top while we watch from the bench. Where does that leave us? Kicking, scratching and clawing our way as far as we can? I've been poor and it's not fun. So I'm going to roll over as many people I can to get to the top, and cut the rope to make sure I stay there."

Michelle could see now that Andrea was simply a woman bent on monetary gain, and would probably sell her soul to get it.

"I guess those people you plan to roll over include me?"

"Ha, you're a very smart woman, Michelle," Andrea said.

Michelle's food had arrived, but she was no longer hungry enough to sit at the table with Andrea for another second. She went in her purse and found some cash, a twenty-dollar bill.

"You know what? I don't eat with snakes, especially when they reveal themselves as poisonous. Here's the money for my lunch and a tip. Buy yourself some class."

Michelle got up and walked away without either one of them saying another word.

Hungry and irritated, Michelle drove to the meeting with the president feeling more passionate than ever about landing the lead anchor job. As much as she wanted to take the high road, it was evident that Andrea never would. Now she wanted the job for one more reason, to kick the shit out of the ladder Andrea wanted to climb so badly.

When she arrived at the office, she saw a jug of purified water in the waiting area. She drank two full cups, hoping to keep her mind off food long enough to get through the interview. The receptionist alerted the president that she was there, and he quickly invited her in. Dale Lindsay was a fifty-year-old white man with blond hair and the most unbelievable tan you've ever seen. He always looked as if he had just come back from Florida every time Michelle had ever run into him.

"Come on in, Michelle. It's nice to see you again."

"Nice to see you too," she lied.

Michelle had never forgotten about the proposition Dale made, that had caused the split between her and her last boyfriend.

"Have a seat. Anything I can get you?"

Michelle glanced around at the spacious office she'd never been inside before.

"No, I'm fine, thanks," she said, taking a seat on the opposite side of his desk.

Dale leaned back in his leather recliner wearing a smirk.

"I scheduled your interview first because I wanted to give you a golden opportunity today, Ms. Mitchell."

"Oh really?" She said with a smile that turned into blushing.

"Oh yes. As you may have figured out by now, you're very well liked around here. When the lead anchor position became available, I want you to know the recommendations came pouring in for you like crazy."

"Wow! Really?" she said with excitement.

Michelle always got along with everyone, but she had no idea that her coworkers held her in such high regard. "This is a surprise, I must say."

"Oh baloney," he teased. "You know the camera loves you, and so do we here at Channel Six."

"Well, I'm humbled by your words, Mr. Lindsay."

"Dale. Just Dale. You don't have to be that formal with me."

"Okay, Dale."

"Now, as you know, this job as well sought after and there's thousands of people who'd love to be sitting where you're sitting right now."

"Agreed."

"And I'll be honest with you. This entire interview process could be nothing more than a formality if you play your cards right."

Dale's eyes got all squinty when he made the last statement, which made Michelle's eyes react in the same manner.

"I'm listening," she said with her antennas up.

"Ms. Mitchell, we're looking for someone that's willing to commit to being the face of the evening news for years to come. We have a lot of new segments that will debut in the next sweeps week, and we want the leads to be very involved with the process."

Sweeps week was very important to the network. The ratings during sweeps week can make or break a show or career. The station reviews their ratings and decide what is working and what needs changes. It was the most important and most stressful time of the year for everyone involved.

"I can assure you that I am more than ready to be involved in the process. I live for being involved in the process." She said truthfully.

Dale nodded, and nodded again.

"I believe that. I believe that with all my heart. Michelle, I'm also looking for someone who is willing to go the extra mile. Someone who wants it bad enough to take it."

The words felt like deja vu to Michelle; she had just heard a similar statement less than an hour ago. She didn't want to read anything into, but this *was* Dale Lindsay.

"Are we still talking about the needs of the station, Mr. Lindsay?"

"Why of course. What else could we be talking about?" he said with wide eyes.

"Well, as I stated, I'm more than ready to jump right in and get my feet wet and my hands dirty doing whatever it takes maintain the reputation and the integrity of the station."

"That's what I want to hear. Now we're talking young lady," Dale said excitedly.

"However, I will not do anything that goes against or compromises my own integrity. Just to be clear, and so we're on the same page."

Dale's smile slowly began to wither away into a frown.

"I don't believe we are, Ms. Mitchell. What would be so demoralizing as to cause you to compromise your integrity while working here?"

Michelle was sick and tired of trying to read between the lines in all of her conversations today. She was almost positive that Dale was propositioning her for the second time, without actually propositioning her. Still, she didn't want to jeopardize the job she already had, so she chose her words carefully.

"I'm sorry, Mr. Lindsay, I'm not implying anything. I just wanted a little clarification on how I could help the station in the future by going the extra mile. Can you give me an example of what might be asked of me as lead anchor that I wasn't aware of?"

Dale sighed.

"Thank you for coming in, Ms. Mitchell, and my office doors are always open if you have any questions or you just want talk about anything."

Michelle was more confused now than she was thirty seconds ago.

"That's it? The interview is over?"

"I'm afraid so. I have Andrea scheduled for one o'clock, but I think we managed to cover everything we needed to.

Michelle was fuming as she stood and placed her test reel on Dale's desk. It was almost too obvious not to speak up, knowing she wouldn't make lead anchor unless she was willing to fuck Dale. Her eyes were like to butcher knives as she made her exit.

"You have a good day, Mr. Lindsay," she said before making her way to the door and yanking it open out of frustration.

The first person she spotted in the waiting area was Andrea, sitting there with an almost knowing smirk on her face.

How did it go?" Andrea pried.

"Fuck off!" Michelle said and stormed down the hallway to the elevator.

By the end of an emotionally trying day, Michelle just wanted her ritual of relaxation. First, the gym with her favorite music on her iPod, the sauna, and then a long soak in her cucumber melon bubble bath.

~~~

Jay knew he had Bones on the ropes. After tossing Pistol Pete's body on the front lawn of their spot, he knew Bones and Skip wouldn't be making any money from that location any time soon. After that, he sent Ray Ray and friends to every house they knew about with guns blazing. One night they caught Skip creeping around the house on Mansfield at three in the morning. Ray Ray chased him down an alley sending hollow tips flying past his head, but Skip managed to escape. It was only a matter of time before Jay caught up with Bones. If he stayed in Detroit, he'd end up just like Dontae, as far as Jay was concerned. The war had become a cat and mouse game of who would be the first to be caught slipping.

At first, Jay stayed away from Michelle to keep her from being in harm's way, but each day that went by was like torture being without her. The one night they shared seemed to be embedded in his brain as one the most memorable moments he'd ever experienced. It didn't seem fair that he couldn't have her.

It didn't seem right that something special could end like that when it was just beginning. Jay went back and forth with himself throughout the day as he sat around his home in St Clair Shores laying low. The truth was, the two of them could never work. Their lifestyles and belief systems were just too different, but nothing could detract from the way he felt about Michelle. He looked at the time, knowing she'd be awake for little while longer. He knew he owed her an explanation if he was going to make the call. He had thought about it all day long. He even thought about telling her some half-truths, as opposed to the outright lies he'd been telling from the start. Michelle couldn't handle the truth, not even bits and pieces of it. Selfish or not, Jay couldn't go another day without Michelle, so he eventually gave in to his desire and called her.

"Hello," Michelle answered. She sounded cold just with one word.

"Don't say anything, just listen for minute."

"Okay."

"I need you to understand that I didn't come into your life to play games and bullshit with you. I came to hopefully make a difference in it. But I gotta be honest, the timing could have been a lot better. I've lost some people that were very close to me since we met, and it's really been taking a toll on me"

"I very sorry for your loss," Michelle sympathized.

"Thanks, I appreciate that. And I know it doesn't look good on my resume to lose contact with you after the night we spent together. That night was special to me, and I want a lot more than a roll in the sack with you, ya dig?"

"I dig."

"I wanna make it up to you if you'll let me," Jay finished.

"Well, if you've had some tragedy in the form of losing a love one, you definitely don't owe me anything, but I'm thankful for the fact that you helped me understand. I was a little confused for a moment, but hey..." She shook her head from left to right. "You don't have to make anything up to me, just a simple phone call was good enough for me," Michelle said honestly.

"I'm glad you understand."

"Yes, definitely. Take all the time you need and just--"

"No, I don't need time away from you, we just met. I need time with you. I was thinking dinner at my place Saturday."

Jay knew there was really nowhere he could take Michelle on a date where he would feel one hundred percent secure with her safety unless he literally had Ray Ray and the goons trail them around the entire date. Instead, he opted for some nice quiet time at home with her, where he knew he'd have peace of mind.

"Are you offering to cook for me, Jay?" Michelle said blushing. After such a long day, it was like music to hear his voice again.

"If you ain't never had my Chicken Cordon Blue, you haven't had nothing."

"Are you sure you're up for it?"

"Well, in my mind, once you see what I can do in the kitchen, the game will be mine to lose from there on."

"Hmmm, I'll be the judge of that. Sounds like a date."

"Okay, I'll see you tomorrow."

CHAPTER 19

J ay lounged around his home in nylon shorts and a tank top while the Chicken Cordon Blue baked in the oven. It was the day after Lines' funeral, and he needed a break from it all just to clear his mind and get a sense of what was most important in his life at this point. He woke up thinking of Michelle, and she'd popped in and out his mind all day. He couldn't wait to see her. When the phone rang, he thought it might have been her, but he was surprised to see it was his aunt Jean calling. His aunt had been like a second mother to Jay, which was one of the reasons he and her daughter, Niecey Girl, were so close.

"Hey Auntee," he answered.

"Hey my ass! Why you ain't called me?"

"I'm sorry, I been real busy, Auntee."

"I wish I could come through this phone and knock your busy ass teeth out. You ain't never supposed to be too busy for family. Well, at least not the ones you give a fuck about," she finished. Aunt Jean was always raw and uncut with her tongue; it made no difference who she was talking to. Jay just grinned, knowing she'd never change.

"I'm sorry, it won't happen again."

"Sorry my ass! It bet not happen again."

"Maybe if you didn't cuss me out so much, I would call and come by more often," Jay shot back.

"Muthafucka please, muthafucka please, muthafucka please!"

Jay couldn't help but chuckle as she did her best Bernie Mac impression.

"What's wrong, Auntee, you need anything?"

"Why I gotta need something to call you?"

"Well, usually after you curse me out, you tell me what you need."

"You know what? Fuck you! I been worried about your black ass, that's why I called you. I know you still out there acting like your punk ass daddy, getting into all types of shit. I know it… I been getting bad vibes, Jay."

Jay hated when Aunt Jean got bad vibes. It usually meant something bad was actually about to happen.

"You a little late with your bad vibes this time, Auntee."

"Why? What happened?"

"Lines is dead. He got killed last weekend," Jay informed.

"Lines is dead? Well, when the fuck was you gonna tell me about it?"

"Honestly, I didn't want you to be worried about me, so I was gonna keep it to myself, but I thought you should know. I know you loved him too."

There was a long silence between them.

"Jay, it's time for you to change your life. You know you're like a son to me, and I couldn't take it if something happened to you at my age. You've done what you needed to do for yourself, now it's time to let that shit go. Walk away before it's too late."

This was the first time in all his years of hustling that she had ever come at him like this. It made him actually take a deep breath and consider what she was saying and how much stock he should put in it.

"I'm working on it, Auntee," was all he could say.

"I'm serious, Jay. Don't be like your daddy and get greedy. You get what you can, and get the fuck out! That's how it's supposed to be done. Time's up! You hear me?"

"Yeah, I hear you, Auntee."

"Good. Now when is Lines' funeral?"

"It was yesterday"

"Yesterday?" Aunt Jean shouted.

"Yeah."

"You dirty muthafucka, you know that boy was like a son to me, and you didn't have the decency to call me and tell me he was dead before the funeral?"

"I didn't. I told you I wasn't going to—"

"Let me get off this phone before I have somebody drive me to where you are, so I can beat the shit out of you."

"I love you, Auntee."

"I love you too. Remember what said."

"Okay."

~~~

Michelle pulled into Jay's oversized driveway around 7:30 with the overnight bag he'd made her promise to bring in the backseat. It felt good knowing that Jay was turning out to be the man she thought he was, and not some imposter looking to have a good time. This weekend would definitely be a step in taking their relationship to the next level. You could tell a lot about a person from visiting their home.

She saw Jay's Mercedes for the first time parked all the way in the back. She admired the landscaping as Jay appeared in the doorway and came out to greet her. He peered into the car as if he were looking for something specific as she exited.

"What are you looking for?"

"Your bag."

She giggled. "It's right there," she said and pointed to her back seat.

"Oh, I see it. Let me get that for you."

Jay was casually dressed in jean shorts and a Sean John button down. Michelle wore a long colorful summer dress and sandals. She also wore a long gold necklace with a locket Jay had never seen until that day. Her hair was straight and parted down the middle, hanging on her shoulders. *Oh my God, she is beautiful,* Jay thought as they made their way inside. The way she made him feel was foreign to him.

Michelle looked around at the living room of Jay's house, and was thoroughly impressed by the cleanliness alone, not to mention the elegant décor.

"I see you cleaned up before you invited company," she teased as she roamed around the front of the house.

She came upon the small stone sculpture of an Asian warrior perched on top of the mantel as if he was on guard.

"Does he bite?" she asked.

"No, but as you can see, he has a blade and he's not afraid to use it."

"Uh oh. Well keep him away. I don't trust him already."

Jay eased up close to her and wrapped his arms around her waist.

"You're always safe with me," he said and planted the kiss on her lips he'd been waiting for all day.

Even though Jay had just buried one of his closest friends the day before, Michelle was like food for his soul. She had been able to alter his mood tremendously throughout every obstacle he'd faced since they connected. They both knew the connection they had was a strong one, but it remained to be seen just how strong it could grow to be.

"Come on, let me show you the rest of the place."

Jay guided Michelle through the entire house, showing her what he had done to the place and what was already there when he bought it. Michelle's eyes lit up when she saw the Jacuzzi in the master bathroom, knowing they would probably enjoy it before the night was done. He took her into the game room, which held a full regulation size pool table and a couple of vintage arcade games. After the tour of the house, dinner was served by candlelight, and Michelle was impressed with Jay's skills in the kitchen. Living the bachelor life, he had picked up many things.

"This is unbelievably good," Michelle complimented.

"Oh believe it, ya dig," Jay said as his cell phone rang. It was Dawson punk ass again. He had just left a message yesterday claiming he was just checking on Jay to make sure he was okay, but Jay knew the deal. He was missing the income Jay had been providing over the two years they'd been doing business.

~~~

Although Bones had taken quite a setback with having his operations temporarily shut down, due to the war with Jay, he wasn't hurting by far. He had come home to a major head start, and with the new plug, he and Skip just focused their attention on moving more weight instead of breaking the kilos down. The fact the he had lost valuable people now was eating at him, but he was still eating nonetheless.

Dawson had turned out to be a sweet connect. After dealing with Oshiwa directly the first time, the two met at a hotel downtown, shook hands and began their relationship. Bones thought Dawson was a little arrogant for his taste, but as long as it wasn't directed toward him, he couldn't care less. Today, Bones had agreed to test drive the 500 SL Dawson was letting go for a steal. They met up on the block Dawson frequently did business on, and Bones fell in love with the black on black Benz as soon as he climbed behind the wheel.

"This muthafucka still smell brand new on the inside," Bones noticed.

"Yeah man, I ain't even had it a whole year. I just got too many cars," Dawson said honestly.

"I see ain't no miles on it."

"Yeah, yeah, I don't drive it. I just put the kit on a couple months ago."

Bones pulled off fast trying to get a feel for the take-off. The German engine purred quietly with Jay Z's

"Streets is Watching" on low volume as Bones turned on to Livernois.

Dawson nodded to the music from the passenger seat as they continued up Livernois riding behind dark tints.

"You heard Jay Z new shit?" Dawson finally said.

"Naw, I ain't heard it yet. Is it banging?"

"Yeah. Hell yeah. I got it a couple days ago from right here, matter fact," Dawson said, pointing at Jay's westside location of Damn Good Music. "Hoe ass nigga," he mumbled thinking about how Jay wouldn't return his calls. He only went in the store hoping to catch up with Jay.

Bones caught the disgruntled tone, even if he didn't hear what was said in the mumble.

"I know that hoe ass nigga," Bones said

"Who?"

"Jay."

"Jay Z?"

"Hell naw, Mercedes Jay; the nigga that own that record store."

"Yeah? I know 'em too. We used to do business."

Bones' face went cold at the thought of Jay and Dawson being connected. He gave Dawson a mean mug.

"That nigga killed my brother," Bones said.

"Who? Dontae?"

"Yeah, you ain't hear about it?"

Dawson peeped his demeanor and began to realize what kind of thoughts were running through Bones' mind at the moment. He had no idea the two were enemies.

"I thought they locked the niggas up that killed Dontae?"

"They did, but he beat the case."

"That's what the nigga Jay was going back of forth to court for? Man, baby boy, I swear I didn't even know nothing about it. You know I fuck with Dontae, that was my dude. We made a lot of money together when he was taking them trips to Ohio."

"You still talk to him?" Bones pried.

"Naw, the nigga don't fuck with me no more. I guess he found something better, I don't know."

"Yeah, well, I got twenty stacks for some info on where to find 'em. Meanwhile, he ain't the nigga you wanna be caught in the car with no time soon, you feel me?"

"Baby boy, trust and believe me when I tell you, you ain't even gotta worry about that."

As a matter fact, now that Dawson knew Bones and Jay were beefing, he would be sure to stay away from riding anywhere with Bones in the future as well. Dawson knew bullets didn't have a name on them, and hit men never left the witness alive to tell about it.

Bones believed Dawson when he said he wasn't in touch with Jay, but still, just the realization of how small the circles of the streets were let Bones know he had to come up with a way to end this once and for all, or he'd end up just like Dontae. He couldn't allow Jay to take him out the game.

CHAPTER 20

After a long passionate night of lovemaking that started on the pool table and went to the Jacuzzi and from the Jacuzzi to the bed, Jay and Michelle slept until almost noon. It was the kind of night that could only be created with sexual and mental chemistry at the forefront. The two lay in bed spooning until Jay's phone vibrating on the nightstand finally awakened them both. Michelle rolled out of bed and slipped on her teddy then tip-toed off to the bathroom.

Jay watched her bottom sway all the way out of the room. Just the sight of it made him ready for another round. His dick was in constant craving for her juices. He looked at the phone number once Michelle was gone and saw it was his lawyer calling on a Sunday. He thought it was odd, but it must be important. He quickly called Mr. Marsh back.

"What's the deal, Mr. Marsh?" Jay said.

"Hey Jason, sorry to call on a Sunday."

"Naw, you my man, what's going on?"

"Well, two things. I was calling to let you know I'm relocating my office so I won't be available tomorrow, but I can give you the new address while I got you on the phone. Also, it seems that Keith has changed his contact number. Do you have a number for him?"

"Yeah, he did switch up numbers. I got it though, you ready?"

"Yeah, go ahead."

As he called off Gunner's new telephone number, Michelle came back in the room with the biggest glow in her eyes. He could see she was happy with him.

"What made you move to another office?" Jay asked curiously.

"Just needed more space, that's all. You ready for the address?"

"One sec. Michelle, grab my pad out of that top drawer," Jay said.

Michelle scurried over to the dresser's top shelf and roamed through some junk mail and invoices until she ran across the pad.

"This one?"

"Yeah, it should be a pen in there too."

Moving to the other side of the drawer, Michelle spotted a Bic ink pen on top of an obituary. The face jumped out at her to the point that she had to pick up the obituary along with the pen. As she took Jay the pen and pad, she zoomed in on the face on the front as her mind flashed back to the story.

A hotel.

At least two gunmen.

Overkill.

As soon as Jay hung up the phone, she was there ready with her interrogation.

"Is this your friend that passed away recently?"

"Yeah, that's him," Jay said, sounding mournful.

"You told me your friend died from a tragic car accident. I don't understand why you would lie about something like this." Michelle stood over him with the obituary still in her hand.

Jay sat up in the bed and swung his feet to the floor. He didn't know how she knew, but she knew. "What are you talking about?"

"I reported from the scene of his murder. He was killed in a hotel room along with another man that fell from the third floor."

Jay was at a loss for words. The lies were finally catching up with him, and he didn't have it in him to continue the same pattern that had gotten him there. He took a deep breath.

"I lied."

"Why?"

"Because I didn't ever want you looking at me the way you looking at me right now."

"Right now I'm just wondering why it seems like all your friends are being murdered, and why are you lying about it? What are you not telling me about yourself, Jason?"

"I should have been honest, and I realize that now, but I can't take it back. What's done is done."

"That still doesn't answer my question... you know what? Never mind. It's probably gonna be more lies and bullshit anyway."

Michelle flung the obituary on the bed and stormed into the bathroom with her bag and clothes. Jay didn't go after her because he knew there was nothing he could say at that point that would change the truth. As he sat on the edge of the bed, he tried to think of something positive to say in his defense. When Michelle came out of the bathroom, she was fully dressed and looked as if she had been crying. As she went to grab the rest of her things, Jay blocked her path and grabbed her by the hands.

"Can we talk about this for moment?"

"Let go of me!" she scolded, yanking away. "If a man will lie about something so tragic, then it's hard for me to believe anything he would say to me. How do you pick and choose when to tell the truth, Jason?"

"I made a mistake, but I think I deserve a chance to explain."

"Fuck you!" Michelle spat before turning and quick-stepping out of the bedroom and down the stairs.

Jay wanted to pursue her, but he knew it was pointless. He allowed her to let herself out while he sat on the bed contemplating all the L's he'd taken over the past few months. Sometimes, it seemed like life pulled you up just to knock you back down.

CHAPTER 21

As the days went by, the money poured in with the crew getting back to business and Jay having a steady connect that was beating out all his competitors' prices. On the outside looking in, life couldn't be better, but Jay was miserable and lonely without Michelle. All he had left was his pride, and he'd be damn if he gave that up by begging her to come back. Besides, he was a street nigga, and he knew they were from two different worlds when they met. Nothing lasts forever, he told himself, but it didn't seem fair that things had to end so quickly. At some point, he knew they would have to talk again because Michelle had left her necklace in her hurry to get away from him.

Jay sat at Niecey Girl's house running money through the counting machine with his cousin's help. He finally got tired of holding it all in, and decided to talk to someone about it.

"You know I'm not seeing the reporter anymore," he admitted.

Niecey Girl was not shocked to hear the news. She knew by Jay's demeanor over the past few days that he was down in the dumps for some reason.

"I kinda figured that, because I haven't heard you mention her at all. What happened?"

"I lied to her about how Lines died. Now she thinks I'm a lying piece of shit, amongst other things."

Niecey Girl stopped what she was doing as if she had something important to say.

"You know, I haven't had a man in two years, so I'm never the one trying to give out relationship advice, but it's something I been meaning to talk to you about." She paused for a second to gather her thoughts. "J- Rock is gone, Lines is gone and now Michelle, which I know is the best thing that ever happened to you relationship wise. All of these people are gone because of your lifestyle. How would you feel if something happened to me? I'm not saying this shit haven't been gravy all these years, because I've benefited just like everybody else. But you and I both know the game don't do retirement plans. I think it's time for a change, Jay. I mean, what else do you need? You got plenty of money, legit businesses. What else you need to walk away?"

Jay was stumped by the way Niecey Girl came at him. It was the second time in less than a week someone in his family was telling him to leave the game.

"You been talking to your momma, huh?" Jay said, thinking it had to come from somewhere.

"Not about you. I'm just telling you how I feel. You not just my cousin, nigga, you my best friend, and I couldn't take it if something happened to you. People need you out here, not dead or in jail for life. I just think enough is enough."

"It's not that simple, Niecey, but I hear what you saying. Honestly, I do."

"I hope so. 'Cause I believe life would be so much better if you left the game behind."

~~~

Michelle had flung herself into her work every day since she parted ways with Jay in a dramatic fashion. She was doing all she could to try and erase the magical night they had shared before he had stolen her heart and stuck a blade in it, all in a twenty-four hour turnaround. She convinced herself that Jay was a man she didn't even know six months ago, and it should be almost effortless to get him out of her system. Still, she found herself extremely agitated, because deep down, she knew real feelings had developed between them. Each night for a whole week, she called Leslie and vented to her to keep from feeling sad.

"And do you know this egotistical bastard has not even called once and tried to explain himself?"

"Maybe that's because there is no reasonable excuse for his actions other than the truth, which is probably something you'd rather not hear."

"Exactly. But you know what? The thing is, I'd rather know. It wouldn't change a thing between us, but I'd still rather know the truth, whatever it is," Michelle admitted.

"Well, you know I was team Jason from the beginning, but this sounds like something that really could be a problem in the future. I mean, if he's not who he says he is, then all the trust goes out the window. On the other hand, I think nobody's perfect in relationships, and sometimes you might tell a little white lie for your own benefit. Hell, I know I do," Leslie admitted.

"Yeah, but is this a little white lie or some astronomical fairytale?"

"That remains to be seen. I wish I had an opinion on which road to travel, but honestly, this time I don't. I just want to see you happy, so do whatever your heart and mind can agree on."

"I'm not taking any more advice from you anyway. It's your fault I'm in this mess in the first place."

Leslie gasped. "How dare you!"

"Oh, cut the drama. Seriously, I appreciate you lending me your ear again. Lord knows I hate to be alone with my thoughts sometimes."

"Well, that's what friends are for."

"Yeah, that and coercing you into dating no good men. Okay, I'm finished, I promise."

"You'd better be, heffa."

"I'll talk to you later. I'm going to bed."

"Okay."

Michelle hung up from Leslie and sat on her sofa with the quiet stillness of her home making her feel uneasy. Just as she was getting used to the consistency of having a man in her life, here she was again on a Friday night all alone. Just like Jay, Michelle knew her and Jason had to talk at some point in order to retrieve her necklace, but outside of that, she had no idea what she would say. Nothing left to be said. If anything, he should have something to say. He should have a mouthful to say. She wondered if he was out on a date. Then she told herself she didn't care. She should call him about the necklace right now at eleven pm, just to see if he was on a date or not. Either way, she could set up some way of getting her property from him and moving on. Yup, no time like the present, she convinced herself as she picked the phone back up and began to dial.

"Hello?" Jay answered almost immediately.

"Hello Jason. I was calling you because I left something that belongs to me at your house in my haste to leave."

"Yeah, the necklace. I wanted to call you about it, but I didn't know if you would answer or not, so…"

"Right, well I was just wondering would it be inconvenient for you to maybe drop it off somewhere tomorrow."

There was a long pause.

"Listen, we don't have to end things like this. I think I should at least have a chance to clear up some things that don't make sense to you, and then, if we have to go our separate ways, at least we'll know why."

"I'm listening."

"Not over the phone. Have dinner with me tomorrow."

"I don't think that's a good idea."

"You have to pick up the necklace anyway. I mean, who else am I gonna give it to? Unless you wanna let me keep it as a souvenir?"

"Hell no," she said, but feeling herself being drawn into his conversation more than she wanted to be. "Look, I don't wanna play games, okay? I just want my necklace, but I would like to know why you lied to me."

"Okay, just have dinner with me tomorrow. I have a lot I wanna say, and I don't wanna say it on the phone. I need to look you in your eyes to have this conversation. You wanna know the real? Well I'm gonna give it to you tomorrow night. I know I haven't been that bad of an experience that I don't deserve one last meal."

"Okay, okay. Where?"

"Where else? Your spot, around seven."

"I'll be there."

~~~

Jay arrived at Heaven on Earth early with Ray Ray and company by his side. They grabbed a separate table in the back and sat low key talking amongst themselves. Jay was escorted to a small intimate table for two along the wall. He had decided that if he was going to lose Michelle, it wouldn't be without a fight. The fact was, he knew there would never be another Michelle Mitchell in his life. Maybe he'd find love one day, but he'd never find another Michelle. He knew Michelle was upset, but he didn't know if she was upset enough to walk away from what they had so fast over something she knew nothing about. What he was about to tell her was as truthful as he could ever be with a news reporter from a completely different world with a different set of moral standards. For the first time ever, Jay was seriously considering leaving the game. Not just for Michelle, but for his family and his own future. Still, he had plenty of unfinished business.

"Hello Jason," Michelle said as she arrived at the table looking stunning in a red sleeveless low cut dress.

"Hey, I'm glad you could make it."

"I said I would be here," she said, taking a seat."

"How's work?"

"It's getting pretty exciting. I'm set to do a fill in behind the anchor desk next week. It's supposedly to help the station decide if I'd be a good fit for lead anchor."

"Yeah? That's big. That's what you wanted, right?"

"Yeah, but I'm not getting my hopes up too high. It's a lot of politics that go on behind the scene. But enough about me. I'm here to talk about you," Michelle said, changing her entire facial expression from friendly to deadly serious in seconds.

Jay glanced around, looking at the table Ray Ray and friends sat, then at the floor and back into Michelle's eyes.

"Are you guys ready to order, or do you need a moment?" The waitress said, interrupting Jay's thought process.

Knowing what she wanted, Michelle went ahead and placed her order and Jay followed. The waitress took the menus and left swiftly.

"Michelle, I don't think I've ever met a woman that compares to you in my entire life. I think I just wanted to make it work so bad, that I was willing to get outside of my character in order to do it. It was selfish to lie to protect myself from losing you, but to be honest, if I had it to do over I'd probably make the same decision."

"Lose me? Why would you lose me? What is it about your life that you're not telling me? Just lay it all out for me now, and let's go from there."

"Well, what I wasn't telling you is what you found out. I have friends that live a dangerous lifestyle. Friends that get shot and killed sometimes because of it. I come from the very same lifestyle. I played the cards I was dealt in life, and I managed to get ahead, but not without a price."

"Wait… Are you saying you are a drug dealer?"

"I'm saying, I've done things in my life that a lot of people probably wouldn't agree with, including you."

Michelle grabbed her purse and prepared to make her exit. No way was this the man for her. "This conversation is over. I've heard enough."

Jay grabbed her hand to prevent her from standing up to leave. "Listen. Don't judge me before you know my real life. I'm sure it's easy to sit there and say I was wrong for my life choices, but you've never been in my shoes. Our backgrounds are different, our parents were different, and as a man, I had to find my own way with the only resources I had available."

"You don't understand. I'm currently up for a promotion that would make me the face of the Channel Six news team. I can't date a drug dealer!"

"I'm not asking you to date a drug dealer. I'm asking you to forgive my past and build a future with me."

"I... I pride myself on being a person of integrity. A person with a love for the community and someone who wants to be a part of the positive changes this city needs. Your past goes against everything I believe in."

Jay finally released her hand and sat back in his chair gazing in her eyes. He felt like his world could be crumbling, and at that very moment, there wasn't anything he could say that would change things.

"So let me ask you something. This positive change you see for the city of Detroit; where would it leave someone like me? What do you do? Lock us all up in a cage and throw away the key?"

"We all have to make our own decisions in life, Jason, and we all have to be held responsible. I'll admit you are someone I saw myself building a future with. You're everything I could ask for in a man, except the fact that I can't trust you. I can't even trust you to be around for the long haul. Like you said, people from your walk of life die all the time, and I'm usually one of the people who hear about it first. How could you expect us to work?"

"You didn't answer my question. What would you do with people like me?"

Michelle took a deep breath and thought the question over before answering.

"I think if people are willing to make a change, and not still continue to travel down the same road of ghetto street life bullshit, then everyone deserves a second chance. But I think if you're going to continue down the same path and you're part of the problem, then yeah, maybe you should be put away where you can't wreak havoc on society."

"So why don't you help me with the transition? Instead of running out on me, how about you help me with the change? Help me become a productive member of society."

"Can you?"

"Michelle, I'm not a monster. Come on now, I've done some things in my life, but you should know by now that I have a good heart."

"Maybe so, Jason, but I mean... this is really bad timing even if I—"

"I don't have anything in my past that could come back to haunt you. I've never been convicted of a crime, so as far as anyone outside of the underworld knows, I'm an entrepreneur. That's all I'll ever be known as."

"But this is your life, you just said it. Your friends are your friends, that's not going to change even if—"

"I just need you to believe in me. If you leave now, where's my motivation to move forward with change? Just believe in me, and I promise you won't ever regret it."

Deep down inside Michelle wanted to believe in Jay. She was never the type of person to be easily misled, but she was a woman who believed in second chances. She knew if she went forward with a romantic relationship with Jay, from this point on, it could be life altering and she'd have no one else to blame but herself. She contemplated.

"Can you really see yourself cutting all your ties to your past life?" Michelle asked.

"It's already in the process. I can't change who my friends are, but I can change my ways. But I can't make you believe me, you'll just have to stick around to see for yourself. Will you?"

Michelle leaned in closely and looked him in his eyes. "If you're ever under investigation, I walk. If you're ever arrested in connection with a crime, I walk. If I ever find out that you've lied to me about getting out of the life, I'm walking away...forever."

She was so close to Jay and had just lifted such a huge sort of stress from his shoulder, he was inspired to lean in and kiss her softly. She accepted his kiss.

"I love you girl," Jay said as he remembered he had a pending charge to deal with.

"Apparently, I love you too."

As the food arrived, Michelle looked up and noticed Dawson strolling in with a Puerto Rican dime piece on his arm. She smiled at the mayor's son and his eye candy.

"Hey look, there's Dawson," Michelle said knowing him and Jay were friends.

Dawson saw Michelle pointing his way and noticed her and Jay for the first time. He headed toward their table with his chest poked out proudly. Jay didn't want to see Dawson anywhere, but he definitely didn't want to see him here and now. Jay's eyes danced around in his head as he got up to put on a show for Michelle.

"What's up, baby boy?" Dawson spoke and the two embraced in fake hug after a fake fist pound.

"You got it, you dig. How you been?"

"I been good, man. I been trying to catch up with you." Dawson said, putting him on the spot.

"I know, man. I never did return your call. I been a busy man these days though, blame on it my mind and not my heart."

"Oh yeah, you know I how it go." Dawson turned to Michelle. "How you been, Michelle?"

"I've been great, how about yourself?"

Dawson pointed to his date, making her blush. "I'm doing okay. I got no complaints over here."

"I see," Michelle giggled.

Dawson complimented Michelle on everything from her dress to her smile, trying to ignore the bad vibes Jay was giving off. He introduced his date and Jay spoke flatly, but Michelle was more cordial. Once he saw Jay refused to warm up to them, Dawson cut the reunion short and said his goodbyes.

"Hey, give me call, Jay, okay?"

"Yeah, yeah I'ma call you in the morning," Jay lied.

He couldn't care less if Dawson drove his car over a bridge after leaving Heaven on Earth. His mind was fixed on making good on all the promises he'd just made to Michelle. Now, more than ever, Jay was ready to retire from the game. He had to have a talk with the crew, and he had to find Bones and put him next to his brother, Dontae, in a cemetery.

Jay and Michelle enjoyed their dinner without incident. When they left the restaurant, Jay's security was close behind. Even though they looked completely natural and didn't arouse any suspicions from Michelle, Jay knew he couldn't continue to live that way.

CHAPTER 22

One week later

Bones was laying low at Oshiwa's house getting some oral pleasure and waiting on a call when his cell phone rang.

"Mmmm, watch out," he told Oshiwa as she came up for air and he grabbed the phone to answer.

"What's up, you ready?" Dawson said.

"Yeah, I been ready. Waiting on you."

"Okay, you can head my way. I'm at the spot."

"On my way."

Bones pulled up thirty minutes later on the same block he'd met Dawson on when he bought the Benz from him. He was excited about him and Skip finally finding another drug house they could sell rock from. That meant they could start back breaking kilos down and seeing a larger profit. But Skip was still furious about the attempt on his life only weeks ago, and Bones was growing impatient sniffing for Jay's trail like a Bloodhound. They both knew they couldn't really focus on the hustle full time until Jay was six feet deep in a casket somewhere.

When Bones walked in the house, Dawson was on the phone with someone while he counted money and put it in little neat stacks. He bodyguard or whoever the hell he was supposed to be, stood close by watching his back. Bones dropped the gym bag on the floor and gave Dawson a 'get the fuck off the phone' look.

"Let do this," Bones said, interrupting his conversation.

"Just call me when you close by, baby boy. Aiight, I'll see you in a minute."

Dawson hung up the phone and turned to face Bones. He'd had a lot of time over the past week to think while he waited on Bones to re-up. He had concluded that he needed Bones alive and well since he was quickly becoming a top distributor on the westside, while Jay, on the other hand, was giving him the high-hat. He didn't exactly have a horse in the race, it was all about whoever he was eating with. Since Jay no long provided meals, the choice was easy. Somebody was going to die in this war, and he preferred that the death didn't set him back financially.

"I got some good news for ya." Dawson said.

"Oh yeah? What's that?"

"I ran into somebody you been looking for," Dawson said with a grin on his face.

"Who dat?" Bones said. He was intrigued, although he had a strong inkling of who Dawson was about to speak on."

"Old Mercedes boy," Dawson said, waiting for Bones' face to light up with interest.

"When?" Bones asked in an urgent tone.

"It was about a week ago, but it wasn't something I could talk to a nigga on the phone about, so I just had to wait and see you, you know?"

"Yeah, yeah. Where you see the nigga at?"

"I saw him hanging out with his new li'l broad. And I know how you might be able to catch up with him too."

"Don't talk me to death, spit it out."

"First, let me say this. You got twenty racks on this nigga head, right?" He said looking at Bones as he nodded. "Well, the info I'm giving you now is free. All I ask in return is a little brand loyalty from you and your peoples, you feel me?"

"Shiiiid you had that coming anyway. Where that bitch ass nigga at?"

~~~

Jay waited for the final re-up to have the conversation with the whole crew. He had done a lot of soul searching over the past week, and he was positive he was making the right decision. There was nothing left in the game for him but the same fate his father was dealt or worse. The last run he doubled up his package, knowing that the flip would turn him a profit that would officially make him a millionaire. His lawyer assured him that his Fleeing and Alluding police charge would be nothing more than a misdemeanor with a stiff fine. He had the girl of his dreams and a future as an entrepreneur. It was time to say goodbye to hustling. He decided the best place to make the announcement was at Niecey Girl's house, knowing it would be like music to her ears. Everyone was there that mattered to Jay. Gunner, Bake, E, even Ray Ray.

"So, I told y'all I had something I wanted to holler at y'all about, man, so I'm just gone get right into it, ya dig? This my last run, fellas. After this one, I'm done. We made a lot of money over the years, man, especially me and you, Gunner. We made a whole lot of muthafucking money, ya dig, and um, all good things must come to an end. We lost some good niggas to this shit, and I'm ready to cut my losses, ya dig. I know I can't tell no grown ass men what to do with they life, but like I said, this my last run and I'm out. It's time for me to give my cousin her crib back so she finally get her a man up in this muthafucka, have some kids or something, you know."

"Fuck you, nigga. I can get a man whenever I want," Niecey Girl said with the biggest grin on her face. She was so proud of Jay at this moment for making the right decision.

Gunner clapped his hands together as he was about to speak. "Muthafucka can't even be mad at you for that, my nigga, shit you already won. I ain't quite there yet, but I definitely feel where you coming from. I hope one day we can all walk away from this shit, you feel me?"

Everyone in the room agreed with Gunner except Ray Ray.

"Not me, nigga, I'm in this shit to the day I die. I'm just keeping it one hundred. What the fuck I'ma do besides what I do?"

"Ray Ray, I love you boy, no matter what," Jay said. "You been riding for the team since day one, and you ain't even from Van Dyke, so you gone always be good as long as I'm alive. And soon as you bring me that nigga Bones' head, you got fifty large coming, you dig? That's on everything."

"Man, dogs bury bones, man. Trust me, I'ma catch up with his hoe ass if it's the last thing I do."

"Gunner, I'ma plug you with my man, Hector, and it's on you from there," Jay said. "E, Bake, I hope y'all niggas start working on that strip club y'all talked about, man. With the money we bringing in now, niggas can do whatever they wanna do."

"Yeah man, we trying to make it happen, but a nigga can't do shit looking over his shoulders every day," Bake said.

"You right about that. End of the day though, this my beef and I'm in it until it's over whether I'm hustling or not. I'ma finish that bitch."

~~~

Michelle pulled out of the parking lot of Channel Six studio feeling drained. Today, she had to go to a woman's home and interview her about her six-year-old son who was struck in the face by a stray bullet in a drive-by shooting. Miraculously, the young boy survived, and after several surgeries, he was finally back home with his mom. Although the kid had survived, his face was disfigured, and after getting to know the family it really tugged at Michelle's heartstring to know their lives had been completely altered forever in such a tragic way. She had a couple of errands to run, and the first was to try to make it to the dry cleaners before it closed.

When she came off the cluttered freeway, she noticed an old school Caprice Classic continued to make the same turns as she. She hadn't paid it much attention until the third or fourth turn, but after that, she began to grow a little suspicious. As a familiar face in the Detroit Metro area, it wasn't unheard of for news reporters to have stalkers or people that became obsessed with them. The first year she was with Channel Six, a weather girl had quit her job and moved from the area because of an incident with a stalker.

Five minutes later, the Caprice was still behind her. Just to satisfy her own curiosity, she pulled into a BP gas station to see what the car would do. She never came to a complete stop, just circled around the gas station. The Caprice slowed down and the occupants, two black males looked confused as to their next move. They kept straight ahead and Michelle's heart began to race as she cleared the exit and made a left turn, darting into traffic in the opposite direction from which she came. Now she was almost positive she was being followed, and the thought sent chills through her body to know she could possibly be in danger. She quickly unplugged her cell phone from the car charger and called Jay.

"Hey," Jay answered.

"Hey. I need you to stay on the phone with me for a little while. I think I was just being followed."

Just the mention of possible danger sent a wave of fear through Jay, and he immediately reached for his pistol under the seat.

"Where are you now?"

"I'm on Plymouth headed north. I don't see the car anymore, but it kept turning with me for the longest time, and when I pulled into the gas station, it slowed down, watching my next move."

"Did you get a look at who was driving at all?"

"Not a good look. I saw two black males, that's all I know for sure."

"I'm coming to meet up with you now."

"No, you don't have to do that. I just wanted somebody on the phone with me just in case. I was really
scared for a minute, but I think they're gone now,"
Michelle said, glancing in her rearview.

Michelle stayed on the phone with Jay describing the
car and giving him a detailed account of what happened.
Jay had already decided he would no longer take
Michelle out in public until the thing with Bones was
taken care of. He couldn't afford to put her in harm's
way, no matter how much he felt he could protect her.
Instead, he planned a Bahamas trip since Michelle had
vacation time coming up. She was pleased to know they
would be spending it all on an island far away from
everything.

"There's so many crazies in this world, you just never
know," Michelle continued.

"You ever thought about getting you a gun permit?"
Jay suggested.

"Not really, but after today, I may seriously take it
into consideration."

"I think you should."

"Maybe... I don't know. I'll call you back when I
make it home."

CHAPTER 23

Monday Morning

M ichelle and Jay enjoyed a quiet weekend at his home, which was just what they both needed. After the incident on Friday, Michelle didn't feel safe even at her own home. She pushed it all out of her mind over the weekend, but she did decide that she wanted to get her gun license.

Today was the big day, and she was filling in for Diane Roseborough. She was super excited and everyone who knew her was just as happy to see her career continue to advance. She was surprised to see just how grueling and tedious the process of putting together the major stories of the day was. Things changed in the blink of an eye in the news world, and you could have the whole line up set and ready to go barring any major breaking news, but then breaking news sends everything into a tailspin. She got a chance to get to know Reggie, her co-anchor, whom she'd be working side by side with if she was a awarded the position.

Whether she got the job or not, Michelle was happy. Just being in this position, she knew that it was inevitable that she would get to where she really wanted to be in her career. She tried to look at things as optimistically as possible after her fouled up meeting with the powers that be. Her life was filled with all the things she needed for peace of mind and clarity, and she knew Jay played a major factor in all of it. If that tiger could change his stripes for good, she could truly see a future with him. She eagerly anticipated being away with him in the Bahamas for a week; so much so that she found herself day dreaming at her desk as if she didn't have anything else to do. She was interrupted by a man in uniform with a name tag standing at her cubicle carrying a bouquet of flowers.

"Michelle Mitchell?"

"Yes," she said, eyes widened in surprise.

"These are for you," the man said, handing her a dozen white roses with a card attached.

"Oh my God," she purred, accepting the flowers but going immediately to the beautiful card attached. She slid it out and opened it knowing in her heart who it was from.

They say chances make champions. Just wanted to thank you for taking a chance on me
    LOVE JAY

~~~

After hearing that Mercedes Jay was parading around the city with a local celebrity as his girlfriend, Bones was at the end of his rope with Jay. He thought shit was sweet enough that he could still go on with life as if it wasn't a real war in the street taking place. Feeling like their young soldiers were incapable of handling the task of smoking out Mercedes Jay, Skip and Bones took matters into their own hands by barging into the westside location of Damn Good Music with guns drawn. A lone female customer immediately backed up and reached for the sky, assuming it was a stick up. They approached the checkout counter with guns on display but not aimed directly at anyone.

"Where he at?" Bones yelled at the store manager who was terrified and confused. He held his hands in the air, also waiting for them to ask for money, but they never did.

"I – I don't … Who?"

His female sales assistant came from the back carrying a CD the customer had requested. When she cleared the threshold, the customer was breaking for the door and the manager was being held up.

She screamed.

"Bitch shut the fuck up!" Skip yelled as she took off running back to the stock room.

He chased her down gripping a Tech Nine. She ran until she was trapped in a dead end corner of the room. Skip quickly caught up and smacked the shit out of her, then grabbed her by her weave.

"Please don't kill me. Please don't kill me." She begged for mercy as she was being dragged and forced to walk hunched over with her hair entangled in Skip's fist.

"Where the fuck is Jay at?" Skip asked.

"I don't know, he don't be here like that. I swear!"

When Skip arrived back at the front of the store, Bones was mopping the floor with the manger's blood, pistol-whipping him with vicious precision.

"You trying to protect that bitch? Huh?"

"No! I don't know where he is. I swear to God!"

Bones whacked him across the head again until the man went unconscious and fell limp on the floor. Skip slung the girl to floor right next to the manager.

"Please don't! We don't know nothing," the girl continued to beg.

Bones grabbed her by the throat and punched the pistol into her cheekbone. "Bitch this muthafucka is closed for business, you understand me? Don't let me catch you in this muthafucka again, or I'ma leave you right here."

"Okay, okay. I'll never come back. Never ever," the girl promised.

Skip backed up into the middle of the floor and began spraying bullets in every direction, destroying the entire inventory until he was completely out of bullets. When done, they fled the store, leaving an unconscious manager and a petrified sales clerk to relay what happened to Jay.

~~~

Jay was at the Van Dyke location of Damn Good Music when he received the call about what had just happened at the other store. The worst part of it all was that the customer who was in the store had ran outside and called the police once she was out of harm's way. Now his business would more than likely become the target of an investigation. Bones had really hit Jay where it hurt, without laying a hand on him. Although no one was dead, police still turned the store into a crime scene with more than a dozen officers in and outside the store, and they all wanted the answer to the same question. Where was the store owner?

Jay knew that talking to the police about what happened was an impossibility because he had no reasonable explanation that would suffice. Meantime, he knew he needed to get everything cleaned out of the eastside location that didn't belong, in case police showed up there.

He had Gunner remove some digital scales, guns and ammo while he while continued to try to reach Dan Marsh, hoping he could give him a clue as to how to handle the police. The store manager was hurt pretty badly, and while he went into surgery at the hospital, the sales clerk, Tiffany, continued to try to contact Jay, looking for answers and some clue as to what to tell the police. He felt bad for her, but he stopped answering her calls after he found out what had happened. Until he talked to his lawyer, Jay wouldn't say anything to anyone about any of it.

Jay drove through the city with his mind racing a million miles a minute, trying to grasp the full scope of what had happened. This could ruin everything. Everything.

CHAPTER 24

As the stories of the day came rolling in, it was all the good, bad and ugly that Michelle was used to seeing. A young woman mauled by a stray pit bull, a local musician pays for a struggling mom to move into a new home after mold was found in her basement. There would be a meeting in about an hour to finalize what stories would make the cut and in what order.

Reggie, her co-anchor, appeared at her cubicle taking her attention away from the phone call she was on. She held up one finger as she ended the call.

"What's up, Reggie?"

"Uh… I just got a call about a really crazy incident that took place in a record store on Livernois, but my plate is so full at the moment, I can't even begin to investigate. So, I was wondering if you wanted to—"

"What's the name of the record store?" Michelle asked, cutting him off. She knew Jay had a store location in that area and she prayed it had nothing to do with him.

"Damn Good Music, I think was the name. Something about some guys shooting up the store. I have some notes at my desk if you wanna take a look."

"Yes please," Michelle said as panic tried to take over her thought process. The first thing she did was grab the phone to call Jay, but as she dialed the number, Reggie appeared again with the notes. She hung up the phone.

"That's all I have on it, but there's a number for the store on the back."

"Okay. Thanks Reggie."

Michelle held the dial tone button on her desk phone waiting for Reggie to walk away. As soon as he was gone, she dialed the number and her hands were visibly shaking as all the worst possibilities began to surface. Michelle couldn't believe she had fallen for Jay's lies and bullshit again. As the phone rang, she didn't know if she was more worried or upset. He didn't answer and she banged the phone down on the receiver. Seconds later, she picked up and called him again. No answer. She was becoming angry until she realized she was calling him from the job phone, and he wouldn't recognize the number. She reached in her purse, retrieved her cell phone, and dialed his number again. Jay still would not answer and she began to fear the worse. If something was wrong with him, she would not be able to function on the job. She just needed to know that he was okay, and she could be upset later.

She finally looked at the notes Reggie had set on her desk and quickly realized Jay's name was nowhere in the incident report, but it sounded as if the vicious attack was aimed directly at him. She took a deep breath as tears began to well up in her eyes. How could she be so stupid as to trust this man with her heart?

~~~

Jay had finally come to the realization that he needed to let Michelle go. She didn't deserve this life, and he wasn't about to continue trying to lie his way into her good graces. As long as he had this beef simmering in the streets, she would always be in danger with him. When she called, he didn't answer the phone because he felt in his heart that she already knew what had happened, and she would want answers just like everyone else; answers he simply didn't have. He was tired of the lying and tired of trying to make something work that just simply wasn't meant to be.

When he finally got in touch with his lawyer, Dan assured him that going in and talking to the police was the only way to keep them from further harassing him.

He assured Jay that he wouldn't have to incriminate himself or offer any information about the incident, but just showing up and pretending that he was willing to cooperate would suit him a lot better than running and hiding out.

That afternoon, about five hours after the incident took place, Jay got lawyered up and went in to the precinct to talk with the investigating officers. The meeting was a short one because Jay basically said he didn't know why anyone would be looking for him and that he believed the situation was a case of mistaken identity. He told police he'd be getting security cameras installed in the store in the very near future. Dan wouldn't allow any incriminating questions to be answered, and before long, they were out of the precinct and going their separate ways.

As they walked to their cars in the parking lot, Dan hit the alarm on his Cadillac and said, "Jay, I want you to be safe out here. I feel in my heart you're a good guy, but maybe it's time to really think about your future."

If only Dan knew how hard he was trying to do exactly that.

"Thanks, Dan. I understand where you coming from." Jay returned.

~~~

Michelle sat behind the anchor desk trying her best to hold it together. What was supposed to be a shining moment in her career felt like a bad dream that she couldn't wait to wake up from. Not only was Jay not the person he had claimed to be from the beginning, it seemed as if he was willing to endanger the lives of everyone around him for his own personal benefit. He wasn't even man enough to pick up the phone and offer a bullshit explanation about the events that had taken place. Everything she had learned about the incident, she had to learn from doing her job as a reporter. Minutes away from going live on the evening news, she was still blinking away tears, as she could not fathom what this would have done to her career if it was found out that she was involved with a man like Jay.

As the countdown to go live began, she tried her best to regroup and focus on the task at hand, knowing she had so many people rooting for her. The evening news always started with the most dramatic and high profile stories of the day. There was a high profile case of a man charged with a triple homicide, who was finally getting his first day in court. They started with live shots of the man who appeared in court in shackles looking wild and scraggly as he was ushered before the judge. Next was an interview with the woman who was mauled by a pit bull. She was in the hospital recovering from surgery but agreed to an interview.

As Michelle focused on the teleprompter, she saw the story she dreaded pop up on the screen. It would take everything in her to keep her composure and push through it. She really wanted to just climb under the anchor desk and hide, but she continued to remind herself that this was her dirty little secret and no one would ever know but her. She cleared her throat and focused as Reggie pitched over to her.

"This next story is very bizarre. Police say two men stormed into a record store on Livernois with guns drawn and demanded to know the owner's whereabouts. They assaulted a manager and a sales clerk, hoping to get answers, and when they weren't given any valuable information, they proceeded to shoot up the entire store. Police say the assailants fired at least thirty rounds in the store before fleeing the scene. The storeowner is believed to be cooperating at this point, but police say the twenty-nine year old owner believes the thugs have mistaken him for someone else. The men were described as two black males in their late twenties and witnesses say they drove off in a black dodge Ram truck."

As Michelle continued to read from the teleprompter, footage of the actual store location from the outside was run. "If you have any information on the suspects, police are asking you to call the twenty-four hour tip hotline immediately."

Michelle managed to wrap up the story like the true professional she was, but the reality of what was going on in her world continued to haunt her thoughts. She zoned out into a blank stare as Reggie went to a commercial.

He could see that something was obviously wrong. "Michelle, is everything okay?" Reggie asked.

She snapped out of her trance. "Yeah. Yeah, I'm okay."

"You're doing fine, just relax," he assured her, thinking maybe she was a little nervous.

~~~

How ironic it was for Jay as he sat at Niecey Girl's house staring at the pain in Michelle's eyes as she reported on his real life that he had been trying to conceal from her as much as he could. Today was such a special day for her, and he had managed to ruin it with circumstances beyond his own control.

Gunner sat on the couch smoking a blunt, knowing what was running through Jay's mind.

"Gotta let her go, dog. Shit too real out here," Gunner said.

"Right now, I wish I never met her. I don't even gotta worry about it no more though. After this, she wouldn't ever fuck with me again anyway," Jay said as he stood and began to pace the room."

"Jay, you gotta handle this shit. It's been going on for too long," Niecey Girl said.

He already had Ray Ray and the squad out on the street searching high and low for Skip and Bones, but just like Jay wasn't so easy to catch, neither were they.

"Niecey, shut the fuck up. Don't you think I know that?" Jay snapped.

Jay never talked to his favorite cousin in this manner, and she knew at that moment that his level of anger was too far to control his temper, so she simply didn't add fuel to the fire by responding.

"On some real shit, though. Everything gotta go on the back burner until this shit is over," Gunner said.

"Hell yeah, everything gotta go on the back burner. Fuck them record stores, fuck that dope, fuck everything until this shit is taken care of," Jay said still pacing. "Shit, ain't nobody gonna work for me in the stores anyway after this. Muthafuckas gone be scared for they lives."

"We need more people on the streets," Gunner suggested.

Jay just wanted to break something. His anger had taken over, and the rational thought process wasn't working at the moment so he stopped speaking.

Just paced.

Back and forth.

Back and forth.

"You know what? I want you to get the word on the streets. I got a fifty thousand dollar tag on both of them nigga's heads. If they ain't dead in a week, it's going up to seventy-five."

Jay realized all the money in the world was no good if you were laying in a casket. He was willing to go broke. If that's what it took to win this war, so be it.

CHAPTER 25

Three weeks later

J ay had to temporarily close every location of Damn
Good Music. Just like he figured, after the incident at
the westside location, everyone knew that working
for Jay could be a life threatening position. When all the
drugs were sold, he didn't re-up, and he didn't introduce
Gunner to the plug. He didn't do anything. He continued
to up the contract on Bones and Skip, which only sent
them deeper into hiding.

Somehow, Ray Ray found out about the rock house
Bones had opened recently. Even though he had no real
proof the house belonged to Bones, he still went ahead
and killed everybody inside. Now neither side could
make money on the streets or move around comfortably
without looking over their shoulders everywhere they
went. Jay knew as long as his crew wasn't out hustling,

they would be on point at all times, which meant they would make it home at night. Michelle stopped calling him after the first time he ignored her calls. He never reached out to her, knowing she probably wouldn't have anything else to say to him. Out of everything he had lost in this war, losing Michelle is what hurt the most, because unlike J-Rock or Lines, she was still here. Still on his television every day, moving on with her life. A life he felt deep down he was supposed to be sharing with her.

~~~

Michelle decided that she would attend the farewell party for Diane instead of sitting at home alone again moping over the past. In the past few weeks, she had slowly been able to come to grips with the demise of her love affair, and was progressing into the belief that there was someone out there for her. Someone that fit into her lifestyle and had an honest heart. Meanwhile, she turned to the things she knew best to keep herself balanced. She went the gym every chance she got, and she stayed busy with work. After having the feeling she was being followed a second time, Michelle went forward with getting a gun permit, and she had just started going to the shooting range once a week. She found it to be thera-peutic with all she had going on in her life.

The farewell party was held at the Marriott Hotel in St. Clair Shores, not far from where Jay lived. On the way there, she was tempted to drive to his house, ring the doorbell, and slap the shit out him if he answered the door. She decided against it and went to the party to say her goodbyes and have a good time. She was thoroughly enjoying the night until Kurt, the general manager pulled her to the side and informed her that the station had decided to go with Andrea Nelson as the new co-anchor with Reginald Hollow. The news really put a damper on her evening.

"Well, I can't say I'm not disappointed, Kurt, but that's life, you know."

"Yeah, I hate to be the bearer of bad news, but I just remember you told me if I knew something, don't keep you in the dark."

"Yes, and I appreciate the heads up. I really do."

Michelle looked over at Andrea and she was absolutely glowing with pride.

"Yeah, she knows," Kurt said, reading her thoughts.

Life definitely didn't play fair, Michelle thought. Not to get the position was one thing, but to lose out to such an arrogant, underhanded snob really hurt. She didn't have any proof, but she was just about positive Andrea had probably taken the president up on his offer and slept with him to secure the job. Being a woman of class first, she decided that she would swallow her pride and congratulate Andrea on her new job. Even though she felt like crap as she thought about how hard she worked, Michelle was always of the belief that what God had for her, no one could take away.

"Well, I guess I should go and congratulate her. Excuse me," Michelle said, parting ways with Kurt.

As she approached Andrea, who was in a conversation with Reggie and a few others, it seemed that her glowing smile turned into a smirk as she saw Michelle approaching.

"Hello Michelle, how are you?" She squealed.

"I'm wonderful. I hear congratulations are in order for you, so I just wanted to come over and tell you I am truly happy for you and I wish you much continued success."

"Awwwweee. That means so much to me coming from you. You know I was extremely nervous about what decision the station was going to make. You're absolutely great at what you do."

"Well thank you, I appreciate that."

"Hey, don't give up. You'll get there. Just remember sometimes you gotta go the extra mile," Andrea said with a cocky wink of the eye.

If Michelle could have choked her without fear of being arrested, she would have. Instead, she gracefully made her exit from the circle of conversation and went into the bathroom to compose herself. Andrea had all but admitted she had fucked her way into the position. She was proud of it. There was no way Michelle could continue to enjoy the night. It was ruined, and she was ready to leave. She hid out in the bathroom long enough for people to forget she was even at the party, and then she snuck out without saying goodbye to anyone.

In the truck, she drove way past the speed limit, cursing and mumbling as her heart sank into her stomach. It just seemed that sometimes she couldn't win for losing. Michelle was grateful for everything she had, but it was never a pleasant experience to have something dangled in front of you just to be snatched away. That's exactly what had been happening to her over the past few weeks. The relationship she'd been waiting for dangled in front of her, and was snatched away. Her dream job dangled in front of her, and was snatched away. She had a right to feel this way, she told herself as her gas light came on.

Michelle had been so engulfed in self-pity, she hadn't realized she was almost out of gas. She pulled into the nearest gas station and fumbled through her wallet until she found the checking card she was looking for. When she got out to swipe her card, Michelle couldn't believe her eyes. There was Jay coming out of the gas station walking directly towards her. Even though it was dark, the gas station was well lit. They immediately locked eyes and began a staring match. Neither could believe how fate had brought them in contact with each other again so quickly after their break up.

Jay didn't know what to say, but he knew he had to say something. He approached her. The closer he got, Michelle just stared without saying a word. As soon as he was in arms reach, she cocked back and slapped him with all her might. He ate it, knowing he deserved it. She gave him another one and he grabbed her by the arms.

"I'm sorry. Look, something happened in my life a long time ago and I'm still paying for it. I didn't mean to play with your heart."

"But you did! You did, and you put my life in danger while you did it!"

A car pulling up and coming to an aggressive stop interrupted the two. Before she knew it, Michelle was staring down the barrel of a gun, but then went flying to the concrete when Jay shoved her as hard as he could. As shots rang out, Jay caught two slugs that spun him around and another in his back before he went crashing to the ground.

Skip and Bones kicked open the doors, and they exited from each side of the vehicle clutching guns tightly.

Jay lay on the ground gasping for air, just waiting for the next bullet to put him out of his misery.

Skip and Bones were so focused on Jay, now that he was finally in death's grip, they didn't even notice a terrified Michelle on the ground rambling through her purse until she came up with the small chrome pistol, aimed and fired. The first shot struck Skip directly between his eyes and he instantly dropped to the ground.

The second shot caught wind, but the third shot got Bones in the shoulders as he aimed his gun at Michelle. The bullet sank into his shoulder breaking the bone, and forcing him to drop the weapon.

Michelle fired round after round while Bones turned to run from cover. Bones caught another bullet in the side before he made it to his car, slammed in reverse and backed out of the gas station wildly. Bones collided with an oncoming car that spun him around, leaving the car folded, and Bones severely injured at the stop light.

Michelle crawled over to Jay who was face down bleeding heavily.

"Somebody call an ambulance, please!" she shouted not knowing if anybody was even there to hear her cry. "Jason? Jason can you hear?" Terrified and shaking uncontrollably, her eyes shot around the parking lot searching for help. "Just hold on if you can hear me. Just please hold on."

The War Report 2 (Michelle's Scandal) Coming soon!

Also available by King Benjamin

CRY BABY
GANK MASTERZ
GANK MASTERZ 2 ALL OR NOTHING
FUNNY THING ABOUT DEATH (A Short Story)

Connect with King Benjamin:
Facebook: Author King Benjamin
Twitter: @kbwordplayz

www.ingramcontent.com/pod-product-compliance
Lightning Source LLC
Chambersburg PA
CBHW072011290326
41934CB00007BA/856